P9-BYW-235

How to Do
Everything™

Microsoft®
SharePoint® 2010

Stephen Cawood

McGraw Hill

New York Chicago San Francisco Lisbon
London Madrid Mexico City Milan New Delhi
San Juan Seoul Singapore Sydney Toronto

The McGraw·Hill Companies

Library of Congress Cataloging-in-Publication Data

Cawood, Stephen.
 How to do everything : Microsoft SharePoint 2010 / Stephen Cawood. —1
     p.   cm. — (How to do everything)
 Includes index.
 ISBN 978-0-07-174367-9 (pbk.)
 1. Microsoft Office.   2. Microsoft SharePoint (Electronic resource)   3. Business—
Computer programs.   4. Intranets (Computer networks)   I. Title.
 HF5548.4.M525C39   2010
 005.5—dc22   2010029398

McGraw-Hill books are available at special quantity discounts to use as premiums and sales promotions, or for use in corporate training programs. To contact a representative, please e-mail us at bulksales@mcgraw-hill.com.

How to Do Everything™: Microsoft® SharePoint® 2010

Copyright © 2010 by The McGraw-Hill Companies. All rights reserved. Printed in the United States of America. Except as permitted under the Copyright Act of 1976, no part of this publication may be reproduced or distributed in any form or by any means, or stored in a database or retrieval system, without the prior written permission of publisher, with the exception that the program listings may be entered, stored, and executed in a computer system, but they may not be reproduced for publication.

All trademarks or copyrights mentioned herein are the possession of their respective owners and McGraw-Hill makes no claim of ownership by the mention of products that contain these marks.

   34567890   QFR/QFR   10987654321

ISBN   978-0-07-174367-9
MHID   0-07-174367-7

Sponsoring Editor Roger Stewart	**Technical Editor** Sean Wallbridge	**Composition** Glyph International
Editorial Supervisor Patty Mon	**Copy Editor** Bill McManus	**Illustration** Glyph International
Project Manager Vasundhara Sawhney, Glyph International	**Proofreader** Carol Shields	**Art Director, Cover** Jeff Weeks
Acquisitions Coordinator Joya Anthony	**Indexer** Jack Lewis	**Cover Designer** Jeff Weeks
	Production Supervisor James Kussow	

Information has been obtained by McGraw-Hill from sources believed to be reliable. However, because of the possibility of human or mechanical error by our sources, McGraw-Hill, or others, McGraw-Hill does not guarantee the accuracy, adequacy, or completeness of any information and is not responsible for any errors or omissions or the results obtained from the use of such information.

To Andrew, Beth, and project blueberry.

About the Author

Stephen Cawood is a former Microsoft Program Manager on the MCMS and SharePoint product teams. Stephen has written a number of books, including *Microsoft Content Management Server 2002: A Complete Guide, Augmented Reality: A Practical Guide, and Microsoft XNA Game Studio Creator's Guide*. Stephen is currently the Director of Community and Support Services for Metalogix Software and lives in Halifax, Nova Scotia, with his wife Christa.

About the Technical Editor

Sean Wallbridge, President and Principal Consultant of itgroove Professional Services Ltd, is a SharePoint MVP and Evangelist. Sean likes to characterize himself as a "SharePoint Jedi" (there are no experts, just those who continue to explore the enormous ways of the SharePoint force), and there is no better way to describe Sean's enthusiasm for SharePoint. In addition to being a SharePoint Server MVP, Sean has a rich background in the Windows world and carries many certifications, including CISSP, MCSE, MCT, and MCSA.

Contents at a Glance

Contents

Foreword

SharePoint 2010 was designed to enable organizations to be more productive by empowering users to work in new ways. As the biggest SharePoint release to date, it contains rich end-user and platform features that aim to deliver the best productivity experience through the browser, Office client, and phone. SharePoint enables organizations to get a return on their investment by helping them to cut their costs and increase their overall productivity. By deploying SharePoint, IT can consolidate various systems and reduce operational costs. As for productivity, this really depends on end-user SharePoint adoption. And while SharePoint has a very familiar Office experience, there's a lot SharePoint offers and it's important to take the time to learn about the different features and scenarios. This book offers end-user education, tips, and tricks that help organizations and users gain maximum value from their SharePoint investment.

There are many SharePoint books that focus on developers and IT professionals, but this book uniquely targets end users. It covers a rich set of scenarios and is a great practical guide for everyone. Beginners to intermediate users will especially appreciate the information that Stephen details. I've had the pleasure of knowing Stephen since 2001 when he was a Program Manager for Content Management Server at Microsoft. I have very rarely met such a person who has deep technical aptitude and laser focus on customer requirements and needs. I can't think of anyone better to write this book.

I hope you enjoy this book as you unlock the value of your SharePoint application and increase your overall productivity!

—Arpan Shah,
Director of SharePoint Technical Product Management,
Microsoft Corporation

Acknowledgments

First of all, thanks to Roger Stewart and McGraw-Hill for giving me the pleasure of working with them on another book. All authors should be so lucky to have such a professional publisher backing them. This extends to Acquisitions Editor Joya Anthony and Project Manager Vasundhara Sawhney. Sean Wallbridge (of itgroove), the technical editor on this project, did a fantastic job and not only assured technical accuracy, but also helped shape the final result.

This book would have been a lot more difficult without the support of Metalogix. I want to especially thank Ivan O'Sullivan and Chris Risley for their support. Also, Sean McCallum helped keep the figures up-to-date as the examples moved from the SharePoint Beta to the RC build and then to the final RTM version.

I also need to express my gratitude to my wife, Christa, for putting up with me as I worked through evenings to get this project done.

Last, but certainly not least, I want to thank my old friend Arpan Shah for writing the Foreword and the section on SharePoint history.

Introduction

When I started brainstorming ideas for books about SharePoint Server 2010, the concept of an end-user book was very appealing to me for two primary reasons. First of all, there are some exciting changes to the end-user experience in SharePoint 2010. For example, the fluent "ribbon" user interface has been added. And secondly—unlike many applications—SharePoint provides end users with both deep and broad options for customization, personalization, and functionality.

As this book is meant for the end user, my goal was to consider how people use SharePoint and then encapsulate these use cases into chapters. However, to make the book useful beyond a single reading, I have added some reference chapters as well. Each chapter begins with a bulleted "How to..." list that provides a summary of the topics covered in that chapter.

- **Chapter 1, "Introduction and SharePoint History"** This chapter provides the back story of SharePoint and introduces the reader to the SharePoint user interface.
- **Chapter 2, "SharePoint Concepts"** The fundamental components of SharePoint are discussed in this chapter. For example, the differences between sites, lists, and items are described.
- **Chapter 3, "Working with Documents"** The focus of this chapter is document management—still one of the primary use cases for SharePoint users. Topics such as working with documents and the content approval workflow are discussed.
- **Chapter 4, "Collaboration"** Various SharePoint collaboration options are discussed in this chapter—including some new features that have only become available with the release of SharePoint 2010.
- **Chapter 5, "Tagging and Taxonomy"** This chapter provides an introduction to the new Enterprise Managed Metadata (taxonomy) functionality in SharePoint 2010 as well as how to use tagging to create a "folksonomy" within your SharePoint user community.
- **Chapter 6, "Publishing Sites"** Publishing sites are becoming more and more popular with SharePoint users. They are being used not only for intranet sites, but also for public-facing websites. This chapter introduces publishing pages and discusses how they can be used to empower SharePoint users to create their own web pages.

- **Chapter 7, "My Sites and Personalization"** This chapter is about personalization. My Sites are discussed as well as features that allow users to tailor SharePoint to their needs.
- **Chapter 8, "Web Parts"** Web parts are nuggets of functionality that can be used on many SharePoint pages, and this chapter will help you make the most of the out-of-box options.
- **Chapter 9, "Customization"** Customizing SharePoint sites, lists, views, and pages is a huge topic among the SharePoint community. This chapter covers many of the ways that SharePoint can be customized without anyone having to write a single line of code.
- **Chapter 10, "Using SharePoint with Client Applications"** The SharePoint web interface has many advantages, but it isn't the only way to interact with a SharePoint server. This chapter introduces some of the rich client applications that you may want to use with SharePoint. Examples include Microsoft Outlook and Microsoft SharePoint Workspace. A couple of examples of third-party client applications are also discussed in this chapter.
- **Chapter 11, "Template Reference for Libraries, Lists, Pages, and Sites"** This is a reference chapter that provides you with a list of all the site templates, list templates, and page types that ship with SharePoint Foundation 2010 and SharePoint Server 2010.

I feel fortunate to have had a front-row view as content management systems evolved from obscure applications (that few people had heard of) to mainstream business requirements that millions of people use every day.

This was an enjoyable book to write and I hope that you will find it equally useful. Have fun, and feel free to contact me through my blog (www.geeklit.com) or Twitter account (http://twitter.com/cawood) if you have any questions.

1

Introduction and SharePoint History

HOW TO...

- Understand SharePoint's History
- Work with the SharePoint 2010 UI
- Identify the differences between SharePoint Server 2010 and SharePoint Foundation

A book called *How to Do Everything: Microsoft SharePoint 2010* has an obvious practical issue. Over its various releases, SharePoint has added a great deal of functionality and has established itself as both an application for quickly deploying websites and a platform for building almost any web-based functionality imaginable. SharePoint Server 2010 users will take advantage of features such as document management, team collaboration, wikis, taxonomy, and blogs. The list of what you can do with SharePoint is long and diverse.

This wide range of functionality makes it difficult to define SharePoint. Microsoft CEO Steve Ballmer recently took a stab at it when he described SharePoint as "a general-purpose platform for connecting people with information." Rather than trying to imagine what all readers might want to do with their general-purpose platform, this book will focus on what's available in SharePoint Server 2010. Once you've been introduced to the features, how you choose to use them is up to you.

The other aspect that will prevent us from covering "everything" is the fact that this book is meant for end users, so we won't worry about focusing on subjects such as SharePoint development or managing a large, distributed SharePoint server farm. That still leaves us with a great deal of material to discuss but before you get your feet planted in the present, we'll start with a look into the past. Arpan Shah, a Director on the SharePoint team at Microsoft, has written the following retrospective section about the genesis and evolution of SharePoint.

SharePoint History, by Arpan Shah

It's interesting to look at how SharePoint has evolved over the years. Most people had their first experience with SharePoint with the 2007 release. SharePoint has its roots as early as the mid- to late 1990s during the dot-com hype. Businesses were very interested in getting websites up as fast as possible, and Site Server, first released in 1996, played a significant role in providing packaged software to the industry. Site Server 3.0, released in 1998, was especially popular and came in a special Commerce Edition. It delivered content and product management capabilities along with search, personalization, and order processing.

The first official branded SharePoint technologies were released in 2001: SharePoint Portal Server 2001 (codenamed Tahoe) and SharePoint Team Services (STS). The first product was positioned as a portal product that helped businesses aggregate corporate information through navigation and search. SharePoint team sites enabled teams to get sites up and running very quickly to organize documents, events, and other digital information. And while both these technologies were great for the scenarios they targeted, they had little integration between them. Customers wanted to use the two technologies in conjunction and provided strong feedback to Redmond that portal and collaboration were very similar and should be delivered on a common platform to give businesses more flexibility.

Over the next few years, the two teams worked very closely together on delivering a common platform. As part of redesigning the architecture, a few fundamental big bets were made: SQL Server as the backend data store and ASP.NET as the development platform. This made sense given Microsoft's focus on its database storage and development platforms. Web parts were ASP.NET server controls that were based on the Microsoft Digital Dashboard design present in SharePoint Portal Server 2001.

In 2003, SharePoint Portal Server (SPS) 2003 and Windows SharePoint Services (WSS) 2.0 were born. While SPS 2003 was licensed separately, WSS 2.0 was licensed as a part of Windows Server. These two products were built on a common base platform, with SPS 2003 offering deep portal and search functionality at its core and WSS 2.0 delivering core collaboration capabilities (see Figure 1-1). Because of the ease with which WSS 2.0 could be deployed, businesses began deploying WSS 2.0 in spades, leading to mass viral adoption.

During the time that Microsoft was designing and building the SharePoint products and technologies in the 2003 wave, Microsoft acquired a Vancouver-based web content management (WCM) company, NCompass Labs, whose flagship product was a content management platform called Resolution. Shortly after acquiring NCompass in 2001, Microsoft released Microsoft Content Management Server (MCMS) 2001, which used ASP technology for creating web pages. The following year, Microsoft released MCMS 2002, which added ASP.NET functionality. MCMS 2002 was a very popular product and was quickly adopted by many enterprise companies for their public websites.

When SPS 2003 was released, MCMS was a popular WCM solution and SPS 2003 very quickly gained momentum and was widely adopted in the enterprise as an

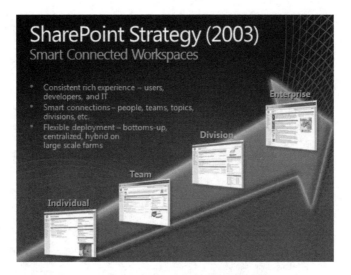

FIGURE 1-1   SharePoint strategy in 2003

intranet solution. With collaboration and portal technologies integrated in SPS 2003, customers were excited about the ability to create team sites and departmental solutions on the same platform.

With the successful delivery of collaboration and portal technologies in one product, the primary customer and partner feedback to Microsoft was to deliver a platform that combined collaboration, portal, and WCM technologies.

In 2004, to address customer and partner feedback, Microsoft released the Microsoft Content Management Server Connector for SharePoint Technologies (codenamed "Spark"). Spark consisted of code and prescriptive architecture guidance that helped customers with some integrated portal and WCM scenarios; for example, customers could use SPS 2003 as their WCM site search engine, and surface WCM page summaries and links within SPS 2003.

Spark was a stopgap that helped address some customer requirements. But what customers and partners really asked for was one integrated platform for WCM, portal, and collaboration. In October 2006, Microsoft released Microsoft Office SharePoint Server (MOSS) 2007 and Windows SharePoint Services 3.0 (see Figure 1-2).

SharePoint 2007 was built on top of Windows Server, SQL Server, and the .NET Framework, much like SPS 2003. However, SharePoint 2007 heavily leveraged the .NET Framework (ASP.NET 2.0), which was more mature and had rich functionality such as master pages and web parts.

SharePoint 2007 had tremendous business success, with over 17,000 customers, 100 million licenses, 4000 system integrators, and over $1.3 billion a year in revenue. It changed the way customers and partners think about business collaboration. It delivered an integrated platform that featured collaboration, portal, search, content

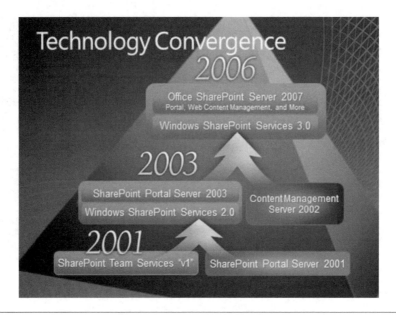

FIGURE 1-2 The convergence of Microsoft technology

management, business forms, and business intelligence technologies. Figure 1-3 represents the integrated capabilities that SharePoint 2007 delivered. By building these different features on a common platform, there was a common and consistent experience for IT professionals and end users. For example, a SharePoint list now stored documents, blog posts, wiki pages, WCM pages, and much more. This meant

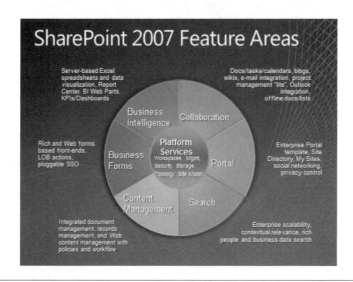

FIGURE 1-3 SharePoint 2007 feature areas

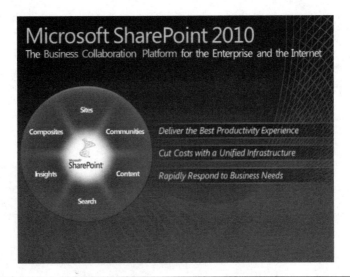

FIGURE 1-4   The SharePoint 2010 wheel

that all the different SharePoint list features, from single-item security to workflow to RSS, accrued to all sorts of scenarios.

SharePoint 2007 not only delivered an integrated set of features, but also delivered top-notch capabilities in each functionality area and was rated at the top of many analyst reports.

In the past few years, Microsoft has continued innovating and making strategic acquisitions to deliver the best value to customers and partners. From acquiring FAST search technology to delivering a cloud-based SharePoint service (SharePoint Online), Microsoft has continuously delivered value while building the next-generation platform for business collaboration: SharePoint 2010.

On May 12, 2010, Microsoft launched SharePoint 2010—the most anticipated release of SharePoint ever. It is designed to deliver the most comprehensive and best productivity experience available today (see Figure 1-4). This book focuses on the end-user experience and the vast set of features that will once again change the way business collaboration is done in the enterprise and on the Internet.

The SharePoint User Interface

SharePoint Server 2010 is a web-focused system. For this reason, the main interface to SharePoint is through web browsers such as Internet Explorer, Apple Safari, and Mozilla Firefox. The main value of a web-based user interface is clearly the "access anywhere" aspect; you don't need to worry about being on a certain computer or installing any software—you can just open a web browser and access SharePoint lists, libraries, and sites. This section explains the main elements that comprise the SharePoint Server 2010 user interface.

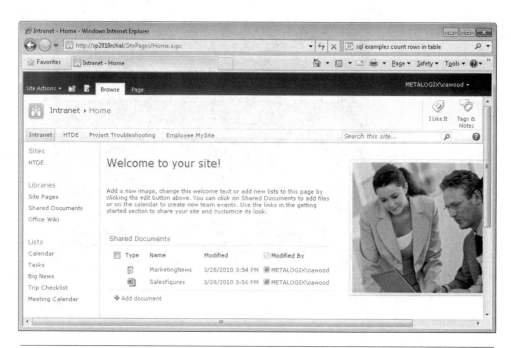

FIGURE 1-5 A standard SharePoint Server 2010 page

Although many people only use SharePoint through this web interface, there are many rich client applications that can add value to the SharePoint experience. Accessing SharePoint from a rich client is discussed in more detail in Chapter 10.

As you'd expect, most SharePoint pages use common elements—for example, the site icon at the top-left corner that navigates to the site's home page, the global navigation at the top of the window, and the quick launch navigation down the left side (see Figure 1-5). Below the quick launch are links to the site's Recycle Bin and the All Site Content page. In the top-right corner of the page, you'll see the search box as well as the tagging options I Like It and Tags & Notes.

SharePoint users will use many of these features daily. To see a demonstration of the SharePoint Server 2010 user interface, you can view this Silverlight video: www.microsoft.com/learning/_silverlight/learningsnacks/SP10/snack02/Default.html.

Sites, lists, and other key SharePoint concepts such as the Recycle Bin are discussed in Chapter 2. SharePoint social tagging is discussed in Chapter 5.

You may not use them every day, but there are other common interface components that need to be covered here. For example, on the left side, you'll see

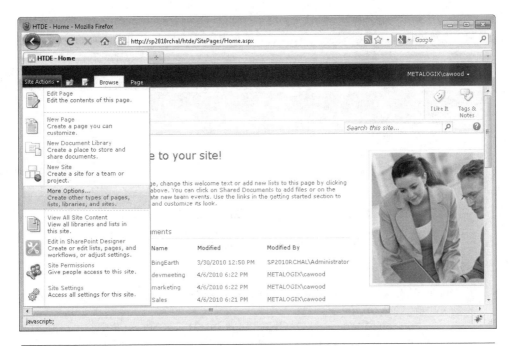

FIGURE 1-6   The Site Actions menu open in Mozilla Firefox

the Site Actions menu (see Figure 1-6). This menu provides such useful links as New Page, New Site, More Options (which leads to the Create page), Manage Content and Structure, View All Site Content, Site Permissions, and Site Settings.

Yet another useful option is the Navigate Up button at the top of the page. This icon, which looks like a little folder and a green arrow pointing up, allows you to see where you are in the site hierarchy (see Figure 1-7). When you expand the drop-down,

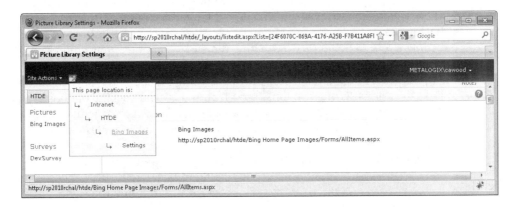

FIGURE 1-7   The Navigate Up button

FIGURE 1-8   The Page tab open in the ribbon

you can click on any of the links provided—in this way, you can quickly jump to another place on the server.

At the top of the page, you'll see that SharePoint Server 2010 pages in edit mode make use of the new Fluent UI (see Figure 1-8). The Fluent UI, or "ribbon" as it's commonly known, was first introduced in Microsoft Office products and is meant to give you quick access to the most frequently used options. In SharePoint, the ribbon provides contextual options, so when you are on a site that contains pages, such as a publishing site, you'll see a tab called Page. If you were editing a page, you'd be offered choices for formatting text, such as bold, italics, and underline.

 Editing pages is discussed in Chapter 9.

However, if you were viewing a list or library, you would see a List or Library tab. In the case of a library, you can switch to the Library tab to see the options available for customizing the library (see Figure 1-9). These options include options for e-mailing a link to the library, switching the view, creating a new column, modifying the current view, or even creating your own custom view.

If you click the link for Library Settings, you'll be taken to a page chockablock full of links to various settings options (see Figure 1-10). The specific options available will vary based on the list or site template and also by your particular permissions. However, options such as customizing the navigation, editing permissions, and creating columns are standard.

If you click the drop-down arrow for a particular item, you will see the options currently available to you for managing that item (see Figure 1-11). These options will change based on the context, type of list (or library), and the rights you have. For example, you might have rights to edit the item or delete it, and if content approval

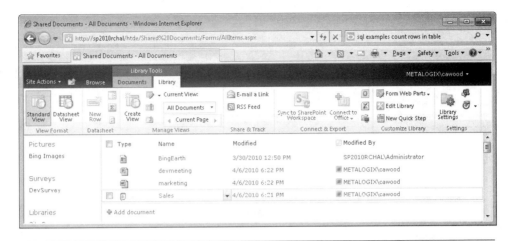

FIGURE 1-9   The Library tab on the ribbon

is enabled, you might be able to check it out, or approve a change. If versioning and workflows are enabled, you might also be able to manage the versions or pass the item through a workflow process.

In the top-right corner of most SharePoint pages, you'll see the username that you've used to log into the server. If you click the drop-down arrow next to your username, you will see various personal options (see Figure 1-12). You can access your My Site, go to your profile page, edit your settings, sign in as a different user, and sign out, and when it's relevant, you'll also see an option to personalize the page.

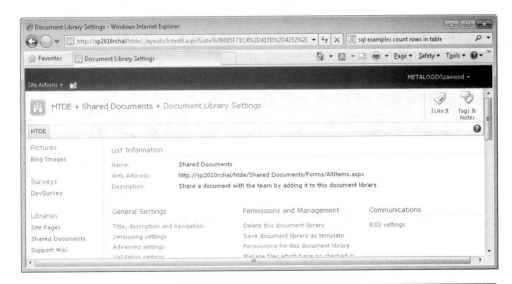

FIGURE 1-10   The Library Settings page for a document library

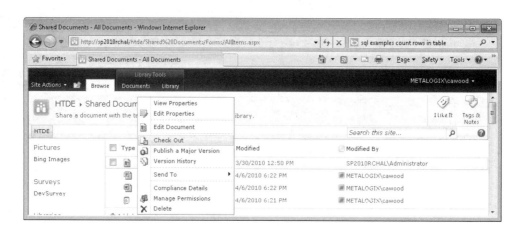

FIGURE 1-11 The item options for a document in a document library

 My Sites are discussed in Chapter 7.

Generally, you'll be able to find the sites and lists you're allowed to view on the global navigation or the quick launch. However, including unique links in these navigation controls is also possible. There could be times when you are looking for a list, library, or subsite and you need some help. Of course, you can use the search box to try and find what you're looking for, but sometimes that isn't sufficient. If you find yourself searching without success, one of the best ways to look is to use the All Site Content page (see Figure 1-13). A link to this page is available at the bottom of the quick launch navigation on the left side, and also under the Site Actions menu.

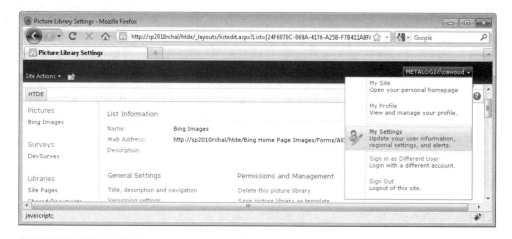

FIGURE 1-12 The personal options menu

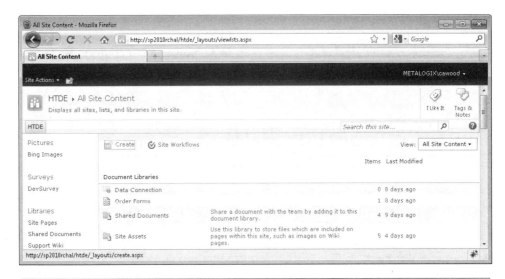

FIGURE 1-13   The All Site Content page in a SharePoint site

 Note   Customizing SharePoint Server 2010 navigation is discussed in Chapter 10.

Navigating around between lists and sites can be time consuming; if you're looking for a more task-centric view of your SharePoint hierarchy, you're in luck. It's called Site Content and Structure. This option will only be available if you have sufficient privileges on the site and the site template has the publishing features enabled. To access this interface, choose Site Actions | Site Settings and then select Content and Structure from the Site Administration category. This opens the Site Content and Structure page for the current site (see Figure 1-14).

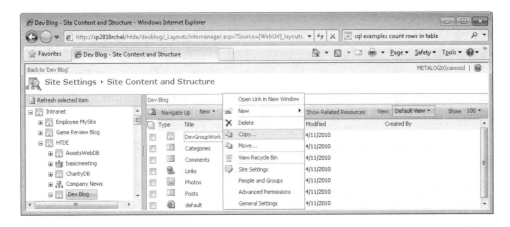

FIGURE 1-14   The Site Content and Structure interface

Site Content and Structure allows you to do some things such as create or delete sites or lists. In some cases, you'll even be able to move or copy them. Using the check boxes next to items, you can make multiple selections to perform some operations on multiple items at the same time—something that might otherwise be quite cumbersome through other means.

SharePoint Server 2010 vs. SharePoint Foundation

SharePoint 2010 comes in two main flavors, SharePoint Server 2010 and SharePoint Foundation. SharePoint Server 2010 is the more feature-rich version and the version targeted by this book. However, if you are using SharePoint Foundation, you'll find that most of this book is still applicable. SharePoint Foundation—as you may have guessed from the name—is the platform that serves as the solid base for the server version. You can think of SharePoint Server as a superset of the functionality you'll find within SharePoint Foundation, but under the hood, they share a great deal.

One way to sum up the difference between the two options is that SharePoint Foundation offers fewer out-of-the-box web parts, list templates, and site templates. However, many people would say that the most notable difference is that SharePoint Foundation is a free download whereas SharePoint Server 2010 is licensed from Microsoft.

In Chapter 2, many of the differences between SharePoint Server 2010 and SharePoint Foundation are highlighted. However, throughout the book various notes will serve to bring these differences to light.

2

SharePoint Concepts

HOW TO...

- Work with sites
- Work with lists
- Work with items and documents
- Use SharePoint permissions
- Work with pages
- Work with web parts
- Use the Recycle Bin
- Use SharePoint Central Administration

The goal of this chapter is to get you familiar with SharePoint terminology and the types of containers, pages, and items you'll find inside SharePoint Server 2010. Unlike traditional websites, you can't look through the directories on a SharePoint server and find the site hierarchy and other assets that comprise the SharePoint content. This is because SharePoint is a dynamic, database-driven application. The site hierarchy is just one example of something that is defined within a database and then dynamically created when a user browses to a SharePoint site.

Inside a SharePoint server farm, the largest container is called a site collection. Site collections contain sites and allow administrators to define permission boundaries and separate resources such as space quotas and features. Since this book is not focused on the administrator's perspective, we're going to skip site collections and focus on what you'll be working with on a day-to-day basis—this includes topics such as SharePoint sites, lists, and items.

Sites

It's not hard to argue that sites are the most important containers in SharePoint. Security is often defined at the site level, and the various site templates determine what type of functionality is enabled within each site. Sure, list templates also define functionality, but sites do it at a macro level.

SharePoint was originally designed as an application for easily building collaborative intranet websites. Over the years, it has grown into a general-purpose platform, but it has also maintained its value as a means to quickly deploy a website. Part of the reason SharePoint can empower uses to create sites so easily is the fact that it provides multiple site templates out of the box. Site templates determine the functionality that comes with a particular type of site. These templates allow users with sufficient rights to effortlessly roll out a new team collaboration site, publishing site, or maybe even a record center.

SharePoint Foundation 2010 includes these site templates listed by category (descriptions from Microsoft are included):

Collaboration

- **Team Site** A site for teams to quickly organize, author, and share information. It provides a document library, and lists for managing announcements, calendar items, tasks, and discussions.
- **Blank Site** A blank site for you to customize based on your requirements.
- **Document Workspace** A site for colleagues to work together on a document. It provides a document library for storing the primary document and supporting files, a tasks list for assigning to-do items, and a links list for resources related to the document.
- **Blog** A site for a person or team to post ideas, observations, and expertise that site visitors can comment on.
- **Group Work Site** This template provides a groupware solution that enables teams to create, organize, and share information quickly and easily. It includes Group Calendar, Circulation, Phone-Call Memo, the Document Library, and the other basic lists.

Meetings

- **Basic Meeting Workspace** A site to plan, organize, and capture the results of a meeting. It provides lists for managing the agenda, meeting attendees, and documents.
- **Blank Meeting Site** A blank meeting site for you to customize based on your requirements.
- **Decision Meeting Workspace** A site for meetings that track status or make decisions. It provides lists for creating tasks, storing documents, and recording decisions.
- **Social Meeting Workspace** A site to plan social occasions. It provides lists for tracking attendees, providing directions, and storing pictures of the event.
- **Multipage Meeting Workspace** A site to plan, organize, and capture the results of a meeting. It provides lists for managing the agenda and meeting attendees in addition to two blank pages for you to customize based on your requirements.

In SharePoint Server 2010, the following site templates are added:

Publishing

- **Publishing Portal** A starter site hierarchy for an Internet-facing site or a large intranet portal. This site can be customized easily with distinctive branding. It includes a home page, a sample press releases subsite, a Search Center, and a login page. Typically, this site has many more readers than contributors, and it is used to publish Web pages with approval workflows.
- **Enterprise Wiki** A site for publishing knowledge that you capture and want to share across the enterprise. It provides an easy content editing experience in a single location for co-authoring content, discussions, and project management.

Custom

< Select template later... > Create an empty site and pick a template for the site at a later time.

SharePoint Server Enterprise Edition

- **Document Center** A site to centrally manage documents in your enterprise.
- **Records Center** This template creates a site designed for records management. Records managers can configure the routing table to direct incoming files to specific locations. The site also lets you manage whether records can be deleted or modified after they are added to the repository.
- **Business Intelligence Center** A site for presenting Business Intelligence Center.
- **Enterprise Search Center** A site for delivering the search experience. The welcome page includes a search box with two tabs: one for general searches, and another for searches for information about people. You can add and customize tabs to focus on other search scopes or result types.
- **My Site Host** A site used for hosting personal sites (My Sites) and the public People Profile page. This template needs to be provisioned only once per User Profile Service Application; please consult the documentation for details.
- **Basic Search Center** A site for delivering the search experience. The site includes pages for search results and advanced searches.
- **Visio Process Repository** A site for teams to quickly view, share, and store Visio process diagrams. It provides a versioned document library for storing process diagrams, and lists for managing announcements, tasks, and review discussions.

My Sites are a special type of SharePoint site; they will be covered in detail in Chapter 7.

Opening a Site

Getting to a SharePoint site is as simple as entering the site's URL (see Figure 2-1). It's important to note that content with any URL under the site (for example, a list URL) is being managed by the settings at the site level. For example, lists and items commonly inherit their user permissions from their parent site.

FIGURE 2-1 A SharePoint Server 2010 home page

Configuring Site Settings

Site templates are one way that SharePoint provides flexibility at the site level, but another key aspect to flexibility is the options in each template's site settings. This section gives you an overview of the various site settings.

To change the configuration of a site, you need to open the Site Settings page. From most locations within SharePoint, you'll be able to access the settings for the current site from Site Actions | Site Settings (see Figure 2-2 and Figure 2-3).

 SharePoint administration options are security trimmed, so if you do not have sufficient rights, you will not see some configuration options.

The options within Site Settings are extensive and many are too esoteric for a book focused on day-to-day SharePoint activities. However, some of them will be covered in other chapters. For the sake of being thorough, here's a list of all the Site Settings options (see Figure 2-4).

Users and Permissions

- **People and groups** Specify users and user groups who have access to this site and any subsite which inherits permissions.
- **Site permissions** Define what capabilities each user or user group can perform on this site and all subsites inheriting permissions.

FIGURE 2-2   The Site Actions button is on the left side.

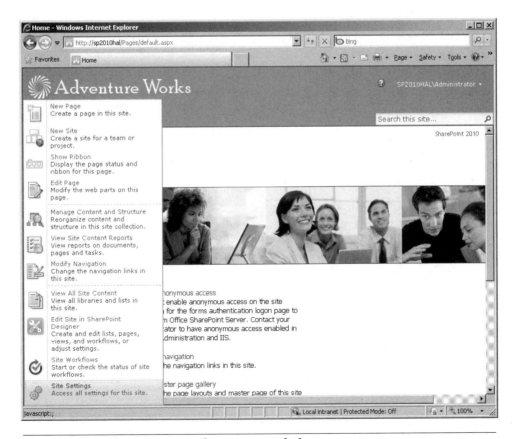

FIGURE 2-3   The Site Actions button expanded

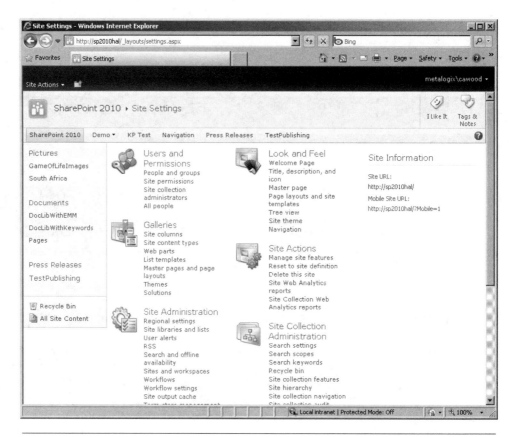

FIGURE 2-4 The Site Settings page

- **Site collection administrators** Add or remove users from the site collection administrators group, which allows members full control over all sites in this site collection. (Available only if you're a site collection administrator.)

Galleries

- **Site columns** Manage the collection of columns available when defining lists.
- **Site content types** Manage the collection of content types, which enables consistent handling of content across sites.
- **Web parts** Select which web parts are available to page owners.
- **List templates** Upload templates that are available when creating lists.
- **Master pages (and page layouts)** Manage the collection of look and feel templates available to sites. (If the site is using publishing features or the collaboration portal template, you will also see "and page layouts" here.)

- **Themes**   Select a style which defines the fonts and colors for this site.
- **Solutions**   Upload and manage solutions, which can contain additional functionality and templates for sites.

Site Administration

- **Regional settings**   Configure regional settings such as locale, time zone, calendar format, and work week for this site.
- **Site libraries and lists**   View and customize the lists and libraries in this site.
- **User alerts**   Manage alert settings for site users.
- **RSS**   Enable or disable syndication feeds for this site.
- **Search and offline availability**   Define whether this site should appear in search results and how search should handle pages with advanced security restrictions.
- **Sites and workspaces**   Review and create subsites and workspaces.
- **Workflows**   Review workflow usage across sites.
- **Workflow settings**   Manage the workflows that are associated with this site.
- **Site output cache**   Configure cache profiles for this publishing site, which allow for performance optimization and reduced page load time. (Available for publishing sites.)
- **Related links scope settings**   Provide sites to be included with the "This and Related Sites" scope of the search results for this site.
- **Term store management**   Manage taxonomy metadata and keyword used by this site.

Look and Feel

- **Welcome page**   Specify the default page for this site. (Available for publishing sites.)
- **Title, description, and icon**   Configure the title, description, and icon displayed on this site.
- **Quick launch**   Manage the links on the quick launch (within a site). (Available for sites other than publishing.)
- **Top link bar**   Manage the links for global navigation (across sites). (Available for sites other than publishing.)
- **Master page**   Select the look and feel template to use on this site. (Available for publishing sites.)
- **Page layouts and site templates**   Define set of page layouts and site templates available to other sites. (Available for publishing sites.)
- **Tree view**   Show or hide the quick launch and hierarchical tree view of sites, lists, and folders.
- **Site theme**   Select a style which defines the fonts and colors for this site.
- **Navigation**   Manage the links on the quick launch (within a site) and global navigation (across sites). (Available for publishing sites.)

Site Actions

- **Manage site features**   Activate or deactivate features that provide additional web parts, pages, and other functionality to your site.
- **Save site as template**   Save this site as a template, which can be reused when creating other sites. (If site publishing is not enabled.)
- **Reset to site definition**   Remove all customizations from a single page or all pages in this site.
- **Delete this site**   Permanently remove this site and all contained content. Click to see more information about this operation.
- **Site web analytics reports**   View traffic or content inventory statistics for this site.
- **Site collection web analytics reports**   View traffic, search, or content inventory statistics for this site collection.

Site Collection Administration

- **Search settings**   Configure custom scopes and search center settings for this site. (Available at the root site.)
- **Search scopes**   Define the search space results for queries on this site. (Available at the root site.)
- **Search keywords**   Provide synonym definitions, best bets, and publishing schedules for search queries on this site. (Available at the root site.)
- **Recycle bin**   Restore or permanently remove items that users have deleted on this site. (Available at the root site.)
- **Site collection features**   Activate or deactivate features that provide additional web parts, pages, and other functionality to sites in this site collection. Some features may require activation at the Site Administration level. (Available at the root site.)
- **Site hierarchy**   Activate or deactivate features that provide additional web parts, pages, and other functionality to sites in this site collection. Some features may require activation at the Site Administration level. (Available at the root site.)
- **Site collection navigation**   (Available for publishing sites.)
- **Site collection audit settings**   Configure auditing, which tracks user actions on all sites in this site collection. (Available at the root site.)
- **Audit log reports**   Review available audit log reports, which provide comprehensive event tracking for content activity, security, policy, or other filters. (Available at the root site.)
- **Portal site connection**   Define a parent site which will appear in the breadcrumb of this site collection. (Available at the root site.)
- **Site collection policies**   Manage information management policies, which provide policy statements, labels, auditing, expiration, and barcodes to all sites in this site collection. (Available at the root site.)
- **Site collection cache profiles**   (Available for publishing sites.)
- **Site collection object cache**   (Available for publishing sites.)

- **Site collection output cache**   (Available for publishing sites.)
- **Content type publishing**   (Available for publishing sites.)
- **Variations**   (Available for publishing sites.)
- **Variation labels**   (Available for publishing sites.)
- **Translatable columns**   (Available for publishing sites.)
- **Variation logs**   (Available for publishing sites.)
- **Suggested content browser locations**   (Available for publishing sites.)
- **SharePoint designer settings**
- **Visual upgrade**   Control the user interface of sites under this site collection.
- **Help settings**

In addition to these categories, you'll see some general information about the site on the right-hand side. For example, you can see the Site URL and the Mobile Site URL listed under the heading Site Information.

Creating New Sites

Creating SharePoint sites is probably not something that you'll be doing every day. However, when you first set up your SharePoint server, you'll obviously need to create some sites. You'll need to plan in advance exactly which sites you need and where to put them. Many SharePoint users do not do this and they end up creating sites in an ad hoc fashion as they're needed. This can lead to the dreaded problem of *SharePoint sprawl*—out of control SharePoint servers that grow without a unifying architecture or plan.

To keep the lid on SharePoint sprawl, most SharePoint users do not have sufficient permissions to create or delete sites. However, if you are able to do so, this section shows you how to perform these operations.

To create a new site under the current site, click the Site Actions button to open the actions menu. From the available options, choose New Site (see Figure 2-5).

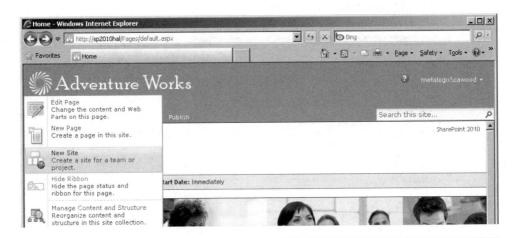

FIGURE 2-5   The New Site option under Site Actions

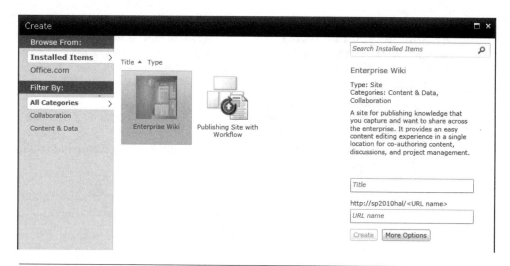

FIGURE 2-6 Creating a new site

The Create dialog opens and asks you to choose from a list of the available site templates (see Figure 2-6). The site template determines the features that will be available within the new site, so it's important to understand what each offers and choose wisely.

 There are third-party SharePoint management tools that will let you re-template lists or sites to a new template. This can be useful when you upgrade to a new version of SharePoint and want to migrate your content to a new template that offers new functionality.

The logical topic to cover after creating sites is site deletion. For SharePoint 2010 publishing sites, the easiest way to delete a site is to use the Manage Content and Structure interface. You can also create a new site using the Manage Content and Structure interface (see Figure 2-7).

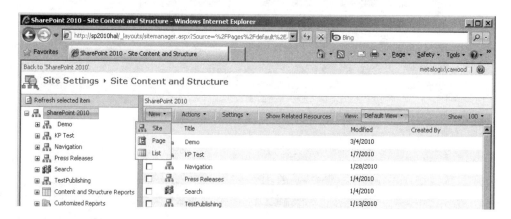

FIGURE 2-7 Creating a site in the Site Content and Structure interface

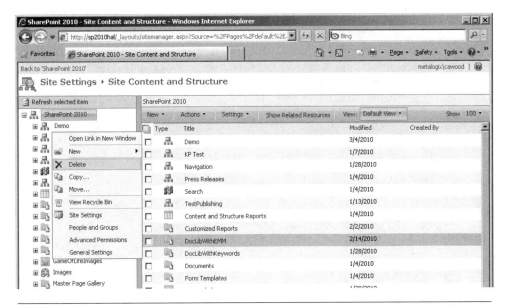

FIGURE 2-8   Deleting a site in the Site Content and Structure interface

Managing Content and Structure

When you're working with publishing sites, there is a handy interface for performing a number of operations. Whether you want to delete a site, move a list, or just see a tree view of your site structure, the Site Content and Structure interface is the place to go. To open the page, choose Manage Content and Structure from the Site Actions menu. If the option does not appear under the Site Actions menu, you likely do not have rights to manage the SharePoint hierarchy.

To delete a site, click the down arrow that appears when you hover over the name of the site and select the Delete action (see Figure 2-8).

You might want to take some time to explore the options available on this page. Understanding your management options will help you decide which decisions about your site structure need to be made in advance, and which you can play by ear.

Lists and Libraries

Sites may be the primary building blocks within SharePoint, but there's no doubt that the workhorses are lists. Lists and libraries contain much of the content within SharePoint, and the list templates determine the sort of information and functionality available to users accessing that content. There are many different types of lists in SharePoint. Some specific types of lists will be covered here and others will be covered in other chapters. SharePoint libraries are special types of lists that have been augmented for particular functionality—you can think of them as lists with attachments. For example, picture libraries have an option to display a slide show of the images in the list. As you'll see in the next chapter, document libraries have a great deal of functionality added for managing documents. Document management is discussed in more detail in Chapter 3.

SharePoint Foundation includes these list templates:

Lists	
Announcements	Calendar
Contacts	Custom List
Custom List in Datasheet View	Discussion Board
External List	Import Spreadsheet
Issue Tracking	Links
Project Tasks	Survey
Tasks	
Libraries	
Asset Library	Data Connection Library
Document Library	Form Library
Picture Library	Wiki Page Library

SharePoint Server 2010 adds these templates:

Status List	Report Library
Slide Library	

Viewing Lists and Library Content

As with sites, any list can be opened by navigating directly to the list URL. If the list has been added to the site navigation, it might be easy to find by navigating to its parent site. However, you can always choose the View All Site Content option from the Site Actions menu and find all the lists that haven't been added to the navigation.

Lists and libraries are displayed using SharePoint views. Some standard views are provided out of the box, but if you need something slightly different, you're free to create your own custom view by clicking on the library tab in the ribbon (see Figure 2-9) and choosing to create a new view. Some customizations, such as which columns to display, can be made quickly using the SharePoint web interface.

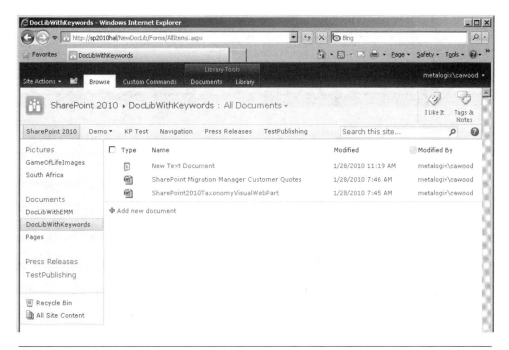

FIGURE 2-9   The default list view for a document library

However, it is also possible to make more substantial changes using Microsoft SharePoint Designer and Microsoft Visual Studio.

If you are looking for something specific in a large list, you might need to sort the data to find what you want. Many of the list columns are enabled for sorting. To use one of them to specify a sort order, simply click the column heading. If you click the column heading a second time, the sort order will be reversed, just like sorting in Windows Explorer. When you choose to sort by a column, a little up or down arrow appears, to indicate that a sort order has been applied to the view (see Figure 2-10).

 Tip   You can add visible drop-down menus to each column that allows filtering by adding ?Filter=1 to the URL of a list. For example, http://server/Shared%20Documents/Forms/AllItems.aspx would become http://server/Shared%20Documents/Forms/AllItems.aspx?Filter=1.

 Did You Know?

You Can Bookmark Your List Views

Rather than going to a list URL and then changing the view, you can simply bookmark the list already in the view that you wish to reuse.

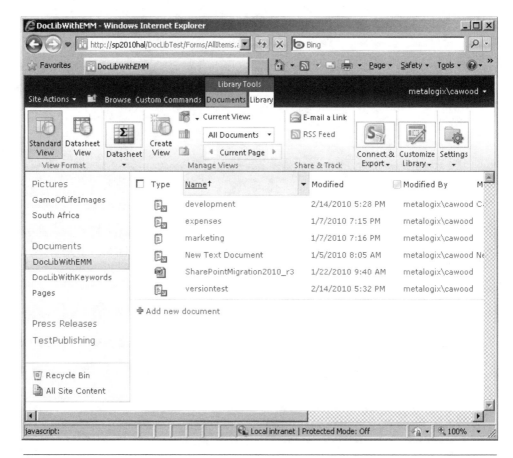

FIGURE 2-10 Sorting by a list column

Sometimes, just sorting the data isn't enough. If the default view does not show you the data that you need to see, or in the format that you need, you can change the list view, as shown in Figure 2-11. Customizing lists is discussed in more detail in Chapter 9.

Configuring a List or Library

In the same way that you can customize site settings, lists and libraries also have many configuration options. When you click Library on the SharePoint ribbon, you'll see the list options that are available to you in the Library section—not every type of list will have this option (see Figure 2-12).

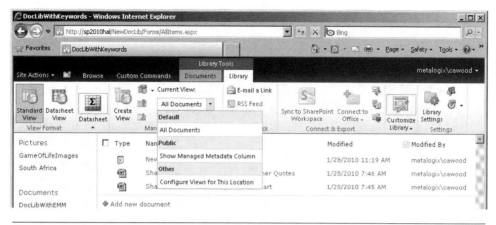

FIGURE 2-11   Selecting a different list view

In the case of a document library, you will be given an option for setting library permissions and adjusting the workflow settings.

Creating and Deleting Lists

If you would like to create a new list under your site, the quickest way to do that is to navigate to Site Actions | View All Site Content (see Figure 2-13).

Once you are on the All Site Content page, there is a Create link at the top of the existing content (see Figure 2-14).

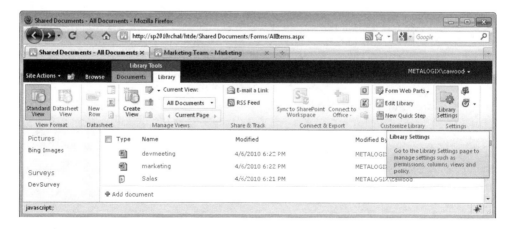

FIGURE 2-12   The Library Settings option in the ribbon

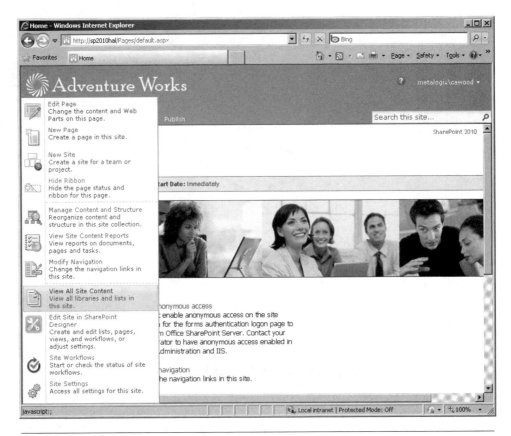

FIGURE 2-13 Selecting View All Site Content from Site Actions

After you click the Create link, the Create dialog opens and gives you the choice of creating the various types of libraries, lists, pages, and sites that are available on your SharePoint server (see Figure 2-15). These choices are defined by the list and site templates that have been installed on your server. SharePoint Foundation users will, therefore, find that they don't have as many choices as SharePoint server users.

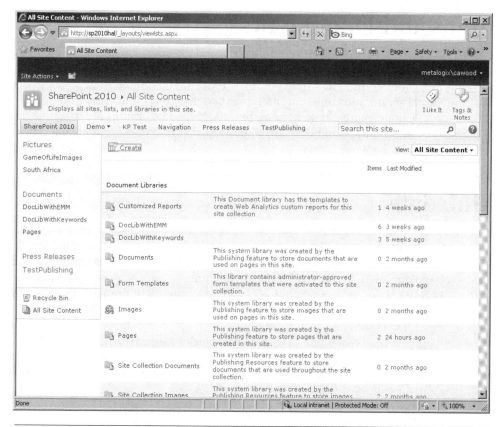

FIGURE 2-14   The All Site Content page

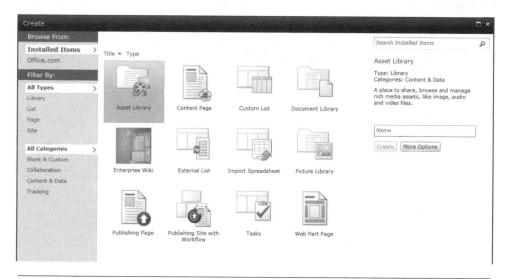

FIGURE 2-15   The Create dialog showing the available choices of list and site templates

Items and Documents

Items comprise the content that fills lists and libraries. For example, the items inside a tasks list are tasks and the items within a picture library are images. Another way to think about items is that they are rows in the SharePoint content database and each piece of information about an item is stored in a column for that row.

Documents are a type of item, but many specific options are available in document libraries, and they are so popular that they receive special treatment in this book; see Chapter 3.

Metadata

Metadata is the invaluable information associated with content in SharePoint. The term comes from the Greek word "meta," which can mean "with." So a simple way to explain metadata is to say that it's information that goes with data, and in SharePoint, that data is your content—documents, lists, folders, sites, and more. However, if you're more technically inclined, you might prefer to think of content as rows in the SharePoint database and metadata as the columns associated with those rows.

Either way, when you look at the properties associated with items, documents, lists, sites or any other SharePoint assets, you are looking at metadata. Examples can include something as simple as the title of a document, to taxonomy data or workflow status—it's all metadata.

Pages

An important aspect of an enterprise content management (ECM) solution such as SharePoint is the web content management (WCM) facilities.

Here's a list of the types of pages included with SharePoint Server 2010. These are used for content management functionality.

- Content Page
- Publishing Page
- Web Part Page

Did You Know?

SharePoint WCM Is Based on MCMS

The WCM features within SharePoint Server are fundamentally based on functionality from another Microsoft product: Microsoft Content Management Server (MCMS). When both SharePoint and MCMS were being developed, there was considerable confusion as to why Microsoft was producing two different products that could be used as platforms for building websites. Having heard the feedback, Microsoft decided to add the MCMS development team to the SharePoint team and consolidate on one platform. They were introduced together for the first time in Microsoft Office SharePoint Server 2007 (MOSS 2007).

Web Parts

Web parts are certainly one of the most fundamental benefits of SharePoint. You can think of them as pieces of functionality that can be added to web pages within your SharePoint sites. Web parts can be used to show all sorts of information. For example, you might choose to show your Outlook calendar or a list of tasks you need to complete. A number of web parts come with SharePoint—roughly 70 come with SharePoint Server 2010, but using the SharePoint framework, developers can write custom code and deploy it to SharePoint as a web part.

Web parts are covered in depth in Chapter 8, but to get you going, this section presents a run-through of how to add a web part to a SharePoint page.

Adding a Web Part to a Page

To add a web part to a web part page, first navigate to a page that you have rights to edit. Once there, choose the Edit option and the page will be refreshed in edit mode (see Figure 2-16).

With the page in edit mode, you'll be able to see the options available to you. On some pages, this will include the ability to add web parts. The visual indication that web parts can be added is that you will see at least one web part zone on the page (see Figure 2-17).

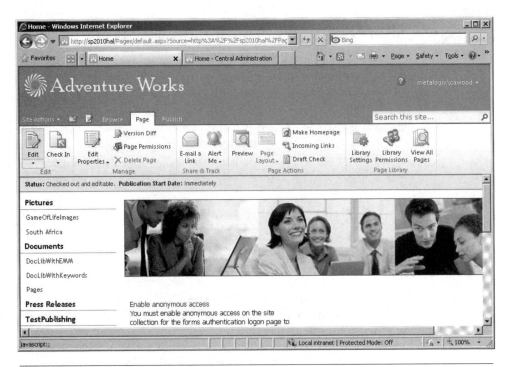

FIGURE 2-16 Getting a page into edit mode

 If you turn on the Wiki Page Home Page feature, you won't be able to add web parts to your home page. Wikis are discussed in more detail in Chapter 4.

To add a web part, simply click the Add a Web Part link within one of the web part zones. Once you click the link, you'll be asked to choose from the available web parts. The options available to you at this point are determined by which web parts have been installed on your server. SharePoint Foundation users will see a subset of the web parts available on a SharePoint Server 2010 server. Also, if any custom or third-party web parts have been installed on your SharePoint installation, these may also appear among your choices. To make it easier to find what you're looking for, the available web parts are divided into categories (see Figure 2-18). The functionality of the out-of-the-box web parts is covered in Chapter 8.

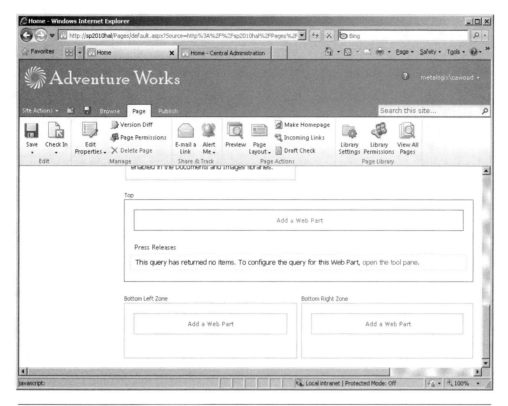

FIGURE 2-17   Web parts can be added into web part zones.

The Recycle Bin

I'm sure everyone has experienced that "oh no!" second that comes immediately after accidentally deleting a file that should not have been deleted. In a feature that is similar to the Microsoft Windows Recycle Bin, SharePoint users also have access to a Recycle Bin. With SharePoint, however, you have access to the Recycle Bin from anywhere because you access it through the SharePoint web-based UI.

The Recycle Bin only stores documents, list items, lists, folders and files. If you delete a list or a site, you will not find it in the Recycle Bin. So long as navigation or quick launch (for nonpublishing sites) is visible, the Recycle Bin is available on all pages (see Figure 2-19).

There are many ways to access the Recycle Bin. For example, if you expand the Site Actions menu and click Site Settings, the Recycle Bin link is also available (see Figure 2-20).

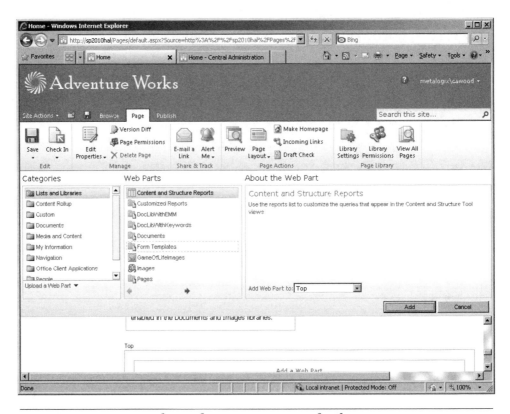

FIGURE 2-18 You can choose from various types of web parts.

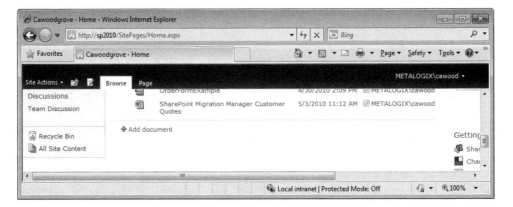

FIGURE 2-19 The Recycle Bin link can be found on the left navigation pane.

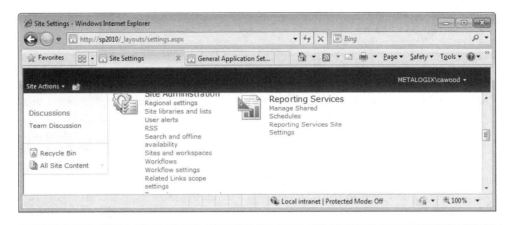

FIGURE 2-20   The Recycle Bin is also accessible from the Site Settings page.

It is paramount to think of the SharePoint Site Recycle Bin as a last resort. Items within SharePoint's Site Recycle Bin are emptied after 30 days, so there is no guarantee that your deleted content will be there when you realize that you need it back.

When the Site Settings page is open, you'll see a Recycle Bin link on the left side. Click this link and the Recycle Bin page will open (see Figure 2-21).

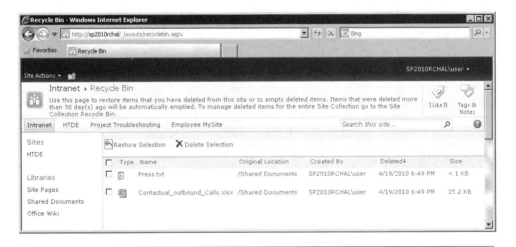

FIGURE 2-21   Viewing the Recycle Bin

Permissions

SharePoint permissions fundamentally define two things: who can see things and who can do things. Permissions can be applied at many different levels, but for ease of management, they are usually defined at the site level. Generally, groups are then used to control which users have rights to each site. This makes permissions for the most common collaboration scenarios relatively easy to manage.

Furthermore, many SharePoint sites, lists, and items are configured to use permissions inheritance. This means that many assets in SharePoint don't have their own permissions applied—they inherit permissions from their parent. This is not only convenient, it is also a SharePoint best practice. While there may be plenty of reasons to define security at the site level, adding security at the list level—or even the item level—can make your permissions management so complicated that you don't really know who has rights to what. To modify the permissions on a site, go to Site Actions | Site Settings | Site Permissions to open the Permissions page (see Figure 2-22).

 Although it is possible to assign permissions to SharePoint items, it is generally not considered to be a good idea. Once you start using permissions other than at the site level, it becomes vastly more difficult to manage and track the permissions of each user.

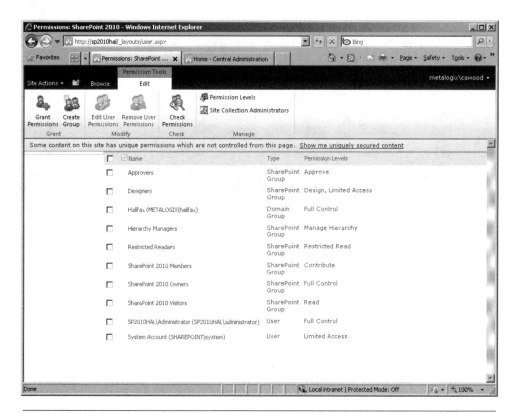

FIGURE 2-22 The site Permissions page, access via the Site Settings page

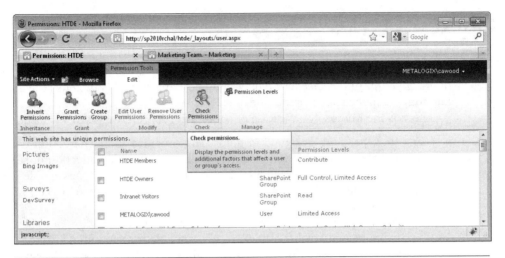

FIGURE 2-23   The Check Permissions option in the ribbon

In SharePoint 2010, there is a new feature called Check Permissions that allows you to go to the settings of a list and quickly see what rights a particular user or group has to the library. To use the feature, go to the library ribbon and click Check Permissions (see Figure 2-23).

After you enter the name of a user or group, the results will show the relevant rights and whether those rights have been granted directly or as a result of group membership (see Figure 2-24).

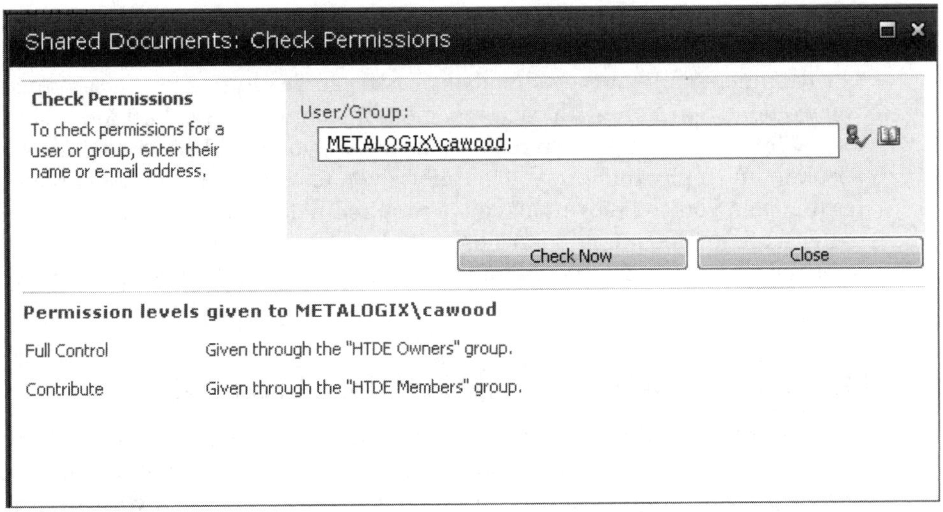

Shared Documents: Check Permissions

Check Permissions

To check permissions for a user or group, enter their name or e-mail address.

User/Group:

METALOGIX\cawood;

[Check Now]   [Close]

Permission levels given to METALOGIX\cawood

Full Control   Given through the "HTDE Owners" group.

Contribute   Given through the "HTDE Members" group.

FIGURE 2-24   Check Permissions results

Content Types

The concept of content types has confused many a SharePoint user, but it doesn't have to be a confusing topic. A content type is simply a way to define a particular set of information. In the case of the document content type, this includes the actual file and some metadata such as the title and filename.

Here is the Microsoft definition of content types from the MSDN website:

> Content types...are designed to help users organize their SharePoint content in a more meaningful way. A content type is a reusable collection of settings you want to apply to a certain category of content. Content types enable you to manage the metadata and behaviors of a document or item type in a centralized, reusable way.
>
> For example, consider the following two types of documents: software specifications and legal contracts. It is reasonable that you might want to store documents of those two types in the same document library. However, the metadata you would want to gather and store about each of these document types would be very different. In addition, you would most likely want to assign very different workflows to the two types of documents.
>
> Source: http://msdn.microsoft.com/en-us/library/ms472236.aspx

Most users do not need to worry about content types. However, it's a good idea to understand that content types can have a parent/child relationship. For example, "document" is a content type in SharePoint, but an unlimited number of specific types of documents could inherit from the document content type and augment it to create a new content type.

If, for example, you wanted to create a "resumé" content type in SharePoint, you might choose to use the base document content type and then add some useful information such as a photo (although that's not allowed in many places, but let's set that aside for a minute), or maybe the current status of the candidate's application. The document content type already has associated columns for most of the metadata you would like to store with each resumé (for example, Title, Last Modified By, and so forth). To add a photo to each resumé in the list, you could add a column that provides a lookup into a picture library. This allows you to associate a photo with every resumé, and you could even make it a required field. You could view your resumés in the standard document library list template, or you could create your own custom template that shows the picture of the person associated with each resumé.

SharePoint Central Administration

While it's true that this book is not focused on SharePoint administration, it would be silly to produce a book about SharePoint that doesn't mention the SharePoint Central Administration interface. "Central admin," as it is usually called, is the hub of all things admin. Using the various settings options, it's possible to perform a mind-numbing number of configuration tasks. These options include backup, migration, security, monitoring, and farm settings.

In true SharePoint style, the administration interface is web based—just like any other SharePoint site. However, for security reasons, the administration interface is often only accessed locally from a SharePoint server.

Opening Central Administration

If you have administrative access to a SharePoint server, you can open SharePoint Central Administration from the Start menu: Start | All Programs | Microsoft SharePoint 2010 Products | SharePoint 2010 Central Administration (see Figure 2-25). Of course, in Windows Server 2008 R2, you can simply go to the Start search box and start typing **SharePoint...**—Windows will fill in your choices as you type.

Here is a rundown of the options available in the central administration interface:

Application Management

- **Manage web applications**   Create and configure web applications.
- **Create site collections**   Create a new top-level web site.

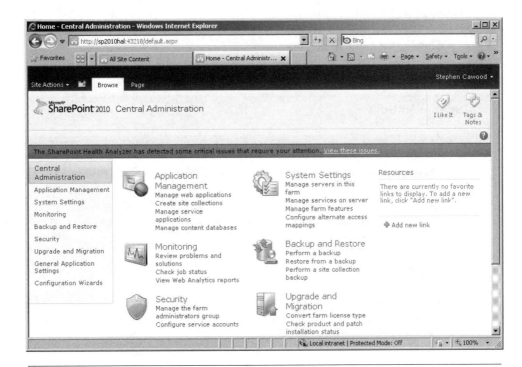

FIGURE 2-25   SharePoint 2010 Central Administration

- **Manage service applications**   Create or manage service applications.
- **Manage content databases**   Add or configure content databases that are attached to a web application.

Monitoring

- **Review problems and solutions**   View the problems detected by the SharePoint Health Analyzer and take steps to solve those problems.
- **Check job status**   View the status and results for the last execution of timer jobs that are enabled in the farm.
- **View web analytics reports**   View traffic, search, or inventory statistics for web applications in the farm.

Security

- **Manage the farm administrators group**   Manage the farm administrators group. Members of this group have complete access to all settings in the farm and can take ownership of any content site.
- **Configure service accounts**   Manage the credentials this farm and associated services use.

General Application Settings

- **Configure send to connections**
- **Configure content deployment paths and jobs**
- **Manage form templates**

System Settings

- **Manage servers in this farm**   Configure and enable services to run on the local farm.
- **Manage services on server**   Select the services that will run on each server in the farm.
- **Manage farm features**   Enable or disable farm-wide SharePoint functionality.
- **Configure alternate access mappings**   Configure the internal and public URL mapping for web applications in the farm.

Backup and Restore

- **Perform a backup**   Back up portions of this farm to a file.
- **Restore from a backup**   Restore content to this farm using a backup file.
- **Perform a site collection backup**   Back up the contents of a site collection.

Upgrade and Migration

- **Convert farm license type**
- **Check product and patch installation status**   View the current product and patch installation status.
- **Check upgrade status**   View the status of current and previous upgrade events.

Configuration Wizards

Although most users don't need to worry about administering their SharePoint server, you may be curious to know a few things from your IT department. For example, how often is your SharePoint server being backed up? Also, what quotas and file limitations are being set on your site collections? You may also want to know how much file storage space has been allocated for your site collection, which file types you are allowed to upload, and what's the maximum file size that you can upload (50MB is the default).

This chapter has introduced you to the various SharePoint concepts that you'll be dealing with in your day-to-day interaction with your own SharePoint server. Working with sites, lists, libraries, and items is clearly a skill that all SharePoint users will employ regularly. While you may never need to know the specifics of content types or how information is stored as metadata, it's always useful to have an understanding of what's happening under the hood.

This chapter also introduced SharePoint Central Administration. Most SharePoint users do not need to administer a SharePoint server, so most users will not have access to this interface. To provide a thorough introduction to SharePoint, the topic was introduced here. However, the goal of this book is to give end users the skills they need for their daily activities, so not many pages in the rest of the book will be devoted to administrative operations.

3

Working with Documents

In most offices, the ability to collaborate on documents is a daily necessity. However, many companies still do not have any sort of document management software. When SharePoint was conceived, this was one of the primary problems the software was designed to resolve. Instead of creating many copies of the same document—and often sending them over e-mail—the idea was to use a common repository that is authoritative and reliable, but also flexible enough to meet the users' needs.

At face value, collaborating on documents from a central store may seem like a simple system to build. But, as with many software problems, the devil is in the details. Offering users flexibility is often in conflict with facilitating features such as a structured content approval process, versioning, and publishing. The complexity of document management was summed up this way in the Microsoft TechNet document *Managing Content with Microsoft SharePoint Portal Server 2001*:

> As an organization creates and collects information, employees spend valuable time searching, organizing, and managing that information. Microsoft® SharePoint™ Portal Server 2001 integrates document management and search functions with the tools you use every day. ... Employees may find large and

complex information sources, such as multiple file shares, difficult to organize and use because there is little or no organizational framework in place. The difficulty increases with the addition of information sources such as Web sites, e-mail servers, and databases. Employees might also have difficulty collaborating with others on documents, controlling access to those documents, and publishing documents in their organization. Important documents can also be lost, overwritten, or hard to find. SharePoint Portal Server offers a number of features to help streamline your document development and avoid these common problems.

To help you manage documents, SharePoint Portal Server offers:

- Version tracking to record the history of documents
- Application of descriptive, searchable information to identify a document
- Document publishing control
- Automated routing of documents to reviewers
- Web discussions for online comments by multiple document reviewers
- Control of document access based on user roles

SharePoint Portal Server helps you collaborate with others, receive feedback from reviewers, identify the document with descriptive information such as keywords, and publish the document to a wide audience.

Source: http://technet.microsoft.com/en-us/library/cc750859.aspx#XSLT section123121120120

Looking at this text, it's clear that the document management goals have remained consistent throughout the many versions of SharePoint. It's also fair to say that, although SharePoint has included document management features since its first release, many end users would still agree that the ability to easily share documents with version control and content approval is still one of SharePoint's killer features.

The goal of this chapter is to cover the most important document management features available from within SharePoint document libraries, and also some functionality available from Microsoft Office client applications. This will help you and your team members start collaborating on SharePoint documents right away.

Document Libraries

In SharePoint Server 2010, the most commonly used central store is the document library. There are many types of libraries, but none are used as often as document libraries because they are custom designed for addressing the complexity of collaboration.

 If you know that you'll be using certain document libraries, you should consider adding shortcuts to those libraries. You can do this by bookmarking the libraries in your web browser or adding them to the quick launch navigation within their parent SharePoint site. You can make this navigation change yourself only if you have rights, so check with your SharePoint administrator to see whether it's something you can do on your own. You can read more about customizing navigation in Chapter 9.

FIGURE 3-1   The new SharePoint ribbon

Opening a Document for Editing

Opening a document from within a SharePoint document library is as simple as clicking the name of the document. Once you click the link, SharePoint asks if you'd like to open the document for editing (if you have rights to edit it) or open a read-only copy.

 When you open a document, SharePoint saves a copy in a temporary file location. This is akin to the way Internet Explorer handles a Microsoft Office document that you open from a website. This usually isn't a problem, because you generally don't want to save a SharePoint document to your local drive—it defeats many of the benefits of having the document managed by SharePoint. However, if you do want to save a copy, make sure that you save it to a location where you can find it later.

Using the SharePoint Ribbon

In SharePoint 2010, libraries have a new user interface (UI)—the ribbon. The ribbon is part of the SharePoint 2010 Fluent UI, and you may recognize it from other Microsoft applications. The ribbon appears along the bottom in Figure 3-1.

 ## You Can Be a Ribbon Hero

Microsoft Office applications (such as Microsoft Word and Excel) were the first to adopt the idea of showing menus in the new ribbon paradigm, but ribbon fever has swept across the Microsoft product teams in Redmond. There is even a Ribbon Hero game (www.officelabs.com/ribbonhero), which collects data while players earn points by using the ribbon interface or working through challenges.

Many of the operations you'll want to perform within SharePoint libraries are offered on the ribbon, so it seems like a good idea to mention it upfront. If you have worked with previous versions of SharePoint, you'll see the benefits right away. If you haven't, you'll have to imagine having to click through a menu of links instead of using the new interface—or maybe you'd prefer to blissfully stay in the present.

 If you're not planning on editing the document, opening it in read-only mode is a good idea because there won't be any chance of you accidentally making a change and then being asked by SharePoint if you'd like to save your changes. This could be invaluable if you had opened the document days earlier and don't quite remember if you intended to make a change or not.

Adding Documents to SharePoint

Before you try some of the SharePoint document management features, you'll obviously need some content within SharePoint. This section covers a few ways that you can get your files into SharePoint and start taking advantage of all the management features as well as general SharePoint benefits such as regular backup.

Uploading an Existing Document

The most common way to get documents into SharePoint is by using the SharePoint web interface. To add a single document to a document library, first navigate to the document library from within SharePoint. Once you're at the right document library, click the Documents tab on the ribbon. This tab gives you access to the most common document library operations, including editing operations, content approval tasks, and publishing options. In this case, you're looking for the Upload Document option (see Figure 3-2).

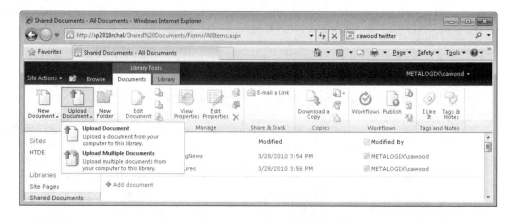

FIGURE 3-2   The document library ribbon with the Upload Document tab expanded

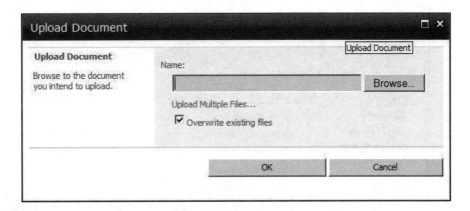

FIGURE 3-3   The Upload Document dialog

For clarity, this book will occasionally refer to manual operations such as check-in and check-out as part of a content approval workflow. You can also create custom workflows for SharePoint Server 2010, but that topic is outside the scope of this end-user focused book. Search online if you're interested in learning about creating your own workflows.

Clicking the Upload Document option launches a dialog that allows you to browse for the document you'd like to upload (see Figure 3-3). At this point, you can click Browse to navigate through the file system and find your document. Also note that you can get to the same Upload Document dialog by clicking the Add New Document link at the bottom of the documents in the list view.

The Upload Document dialog is an example of a new type of dialog in SharePoint 2010. In previous versions, this sort of operation required that the whole page be requested from the server (this is called an ASP.NET postback), whereas now a smaller window opens and then closes to show the original page. Those extra requests to the server—in this case, asking again for the list of documents—had a significant impact on performance.

The Choose File to Upload dialog should look familiar to any Windows user (see Figure 3-4). Simply navigate through the folders on the left, select the file that you'd like to upload to SharePoint and then click Open. You can also skip the last step by double-clicking the file.

SharePoint will not allow blank documents to be uploaded. If you want to upload a test file, simply open the file and add some content to it before you try to add it to SharePoint. Also, filenames cannot contain any of these characters: \ / : * ? " < > | # { } % ~ &.

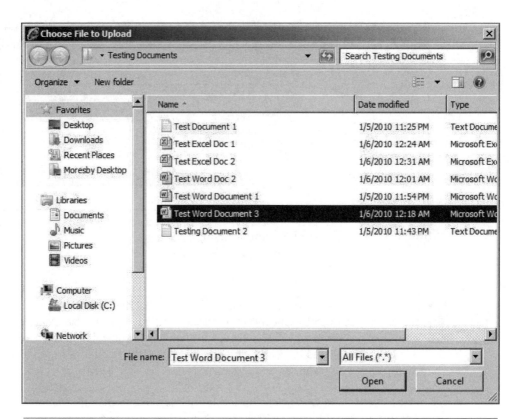

FIGURE 3-4 Browsing for a file to add to a SharePoint document library

After you select your file, you'll be returned to the Upload Document dialog with the path to your file included. Click OK to begin the upload.

 If you already have the file path for your file, you can simply enter or paste it into the Name field of the dialog and avoid the browse step altogether.

It may take some time for large documents to upload. During the file transfer, you'll see a spinning animation to indicate that SharePoint is working on your request.

 SharePoint sites have a setting for the maximum file upload size. By default, the value is 50MB. If your file is larger than this setting, you'll need to either reduce the size of the file or change the setting. If you do not have sufficient rights to change the setting, you need to talk to your SharePoint administrator.

When the upload is complete, you'll be asked for some more information about the document that you are adding to the document library (see Figure 3-5). In the default document library list template, you'll be asked for a mandatory name

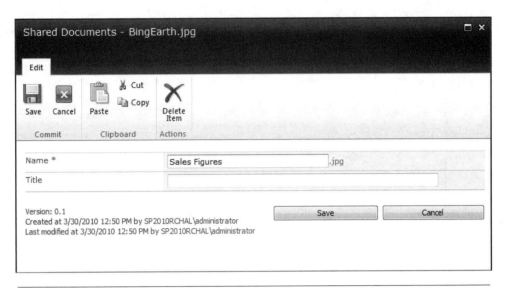

FIGURE 3-5   Adding document properties before upload

(you can use the default value from the file system if you want), and optionally, you can provide a title. The title of the document will appear in the list of documents in the library and it doesn't have to match the filename. In fact, the Title field is specifically provided so that you can use a friendly name instead of a potentially cryptic filename.

After you click the Save button, you'll be returned to the document library, and the list will now include the document you uploaded. In this case, the test document has been added.

This example included many screenshots because it's a great illustration of a standard SharePoint task. Using the ribbon UI and similar dialogs, you'll be able to perform many similar operations and gain access to powerful document management functionality. Of course, uploading files one at a time is not ideal if you want to import an entire directory into SharePoint. For that you'll want to use the Upload Multiple Documents feature.

Did You Know? You Can E-mail Documents to SharePoint

Document libraries and certain types of lists can be e-mail enabled to allow you to simply e-mail a document to them instead of uploading the files through the SharePoint web UI. Speak to your SharePoint administrator if this option is not enabled on your SharePoint server.

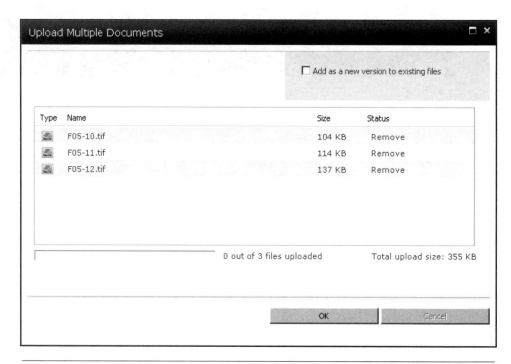

FIGURE 3-6 Browsing for multiple files to upload to SharePoint

Uploading Multiple Documents

While it's possible to upload documents one at a time to document libraries, it's certainly not the fastest way to get a whole directory of files into SharePoint. To upload multiple documents, you'll still select Upload Document from the ribbon, but this time, you'll click the Upload Multiple Files option in the Upload Document dialog, or you can choose the Upload Multiple Documents option in the Upload Document ribbon drop-down menu. The Upload Multiple Documents dialog that opens is shown in Figure 3-6.

In the dialog, you'll see a list of the files you've selected for upload. To confirm the file transfer, simply check the box next to the files you want. When you click OK, your documents will be added to SharePoint. If you choose a folder, the entire directory will be uploaded.

Since uploading multiple files is a more complicated operation, you'll see a different status dialog as the file transfer begins. This status dialog gives you information about which file is being uploaded and how many have already been added (see Figure 3-7).

After the dialog closes, you'll be returned to the document library view that you were previously using and you'll be able to see your new files within the document library.

Clearly, the Upload Multiple Document option is a great time saver. Don't waste your time and effort uploading a bunch of files individually; simply select their directory and upload them en masse.

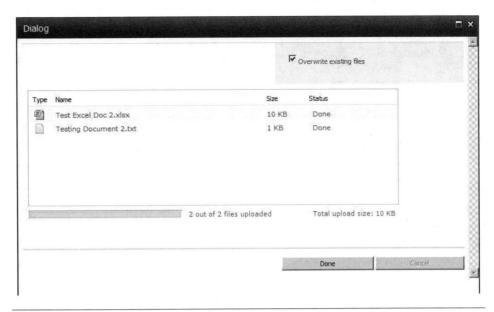

FIGURE 3-7   The Upload Multiple Documents status screen

 Although the ribbon supports Safari, Firefox, and Internet Explorer, Upload Multiple Documents does not work in Safari or Firefox, either on a PC or a MAC.

Upload Multiple Documents only works (like the datasheet view) if you have an Office product installed. If you don't have Microsoft Office, you won't be able to use Upload Multiple Documents, regardless of which browser you're using.

If you have Office 2010 installed (or SharePoint Designer 2010, which is free), you will have the SharePoint Office components installed, and you will have the added ability to drag and drop multiple files into SharePoint. This matrix illustrates the various multiple upload options and what you'll need to use them:

	IE7+ on a PC without Office (2003 or 2007)	IE7+ on a PC with Office (2003 or 2007)	IE7+ on a PC with Office (2010)*	Safari (MAC or PC)	Firefox (MAC or PC)
Upload Multiple, with check boxes	No	Yes	No	No	No
Upload Multiple, drag and drop	No	No	Yes**	No	No

* Office SharePoint Designer 2010 (free) also provides the necessary components for a successful upload via drag and drop.

** As the component comes with Office, not with SharePoint, the drag-and-drop functionality provided by Office 2010 for a SharePoint document library will work the same with a MOSS 2007/WSS 3.0 Server.

Adding Documents with Windows Explorer

It may seem that SharePoint has already provided enough options for adding content to your server, but there are more. The next one is the option to add documents through Windows Explorer.

As you know, SharePoint stores its content within a SQL Server database, so you won't find your SharePoint files if you look through your Windows folders. However, this doesn't mean that you can't use Windows Explorer to quickly get files into SharePoint and copy them out of SharePoint. To use this time-saving feature, go to the document library and, from the Library ribbon tab, choose Open with Explorer (see Figure 3-8).

 To use the Open with Windows Explorer feature, you need to add your SharePoint site to the Local Intranet Zone in the Internet Explorer security settings. Also, Open with Windows Explorer only works if you are using the Internet Explorer browser.

SharePoint launches Windows Explorer and enables you to access your SharePoint content. Once you have the library open, you can drag and drop from your Windows folders into the document library, or vice versa (see Figure 3-9).

 A great time saver is to add your SharePoint library or folder to the Favorites list in Windows Explorer. After you've done this, you can open Windows Explorer and go directly to the bookmarked list. To add SharePoint content to the Favorites, simply drag the item into the Favorites area (see Figure 3-10).

 If you copy a file out of SharePoint using Windows Explorer, you are doing just that—making a copy. The copy will not be bound by any workflow or management features enabled on the source SharePoint library. This is the same caution that applies to saving a copy of a document you opened from SharePoint.

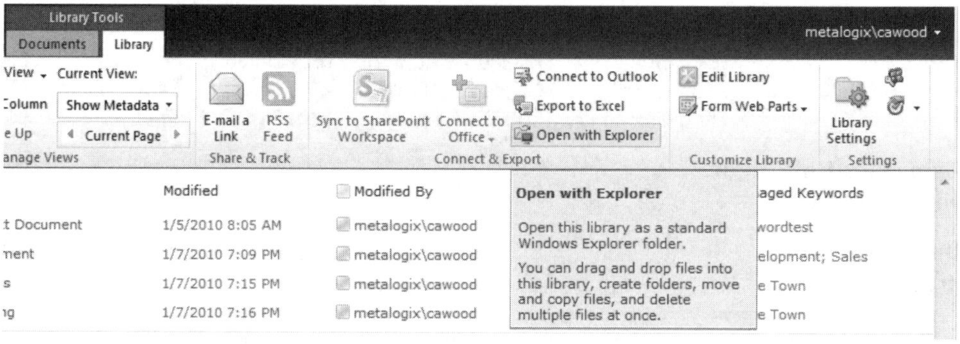

FIGURE 3-8 Using the ribbon to open a SharePoint library in Windows Explorer

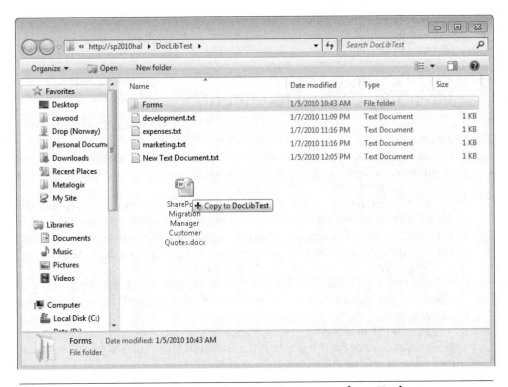

FIGURE 3-9   Dragging a file into SharePoint using Windows Explorer

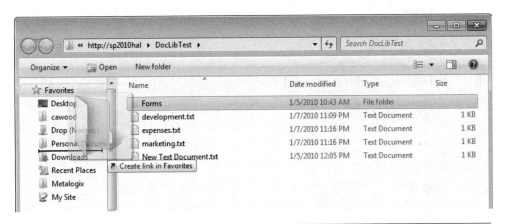

FIGURE 3-10   Adding a SharePoint folder to your Favorites in Windows Explorer

You may be feeling flush with power after seeing how easy it is to copy your documents into SharePoint. Just bear in mind that uploading documents isn't the only way to add content.

Creating a New Document

If you have Microsoft Office installed, you'll also have the option of creating a new document from the document library ribbon. This is useful if you're starting a new Microsoft Office document and you know that you'll be uploading it to SharePoint eventually. Rather than going through multiple steps, you can simply create the file from within SharePoint.

First, go to the library where you want the document to be stored and then find the New Document option on the trusty SharePoint ribbon. This will create a new document using the document library's default document template. For example, if the default template is Microsoft Word 2010, Word will open and allow you to start creating your new document (see Figure 3-11).

You can work on the temporary copy of the document as long as you want, and when you choose to save the file, the client application will ask you to save it in SharePoint (see Figure 3-12).

The choice of whether to first create new documents and then upload them to SharePoint or to begin the whole process within SharePoint is yours. Remember, though, that getting your content into SharePoint as soon as possible often is the best

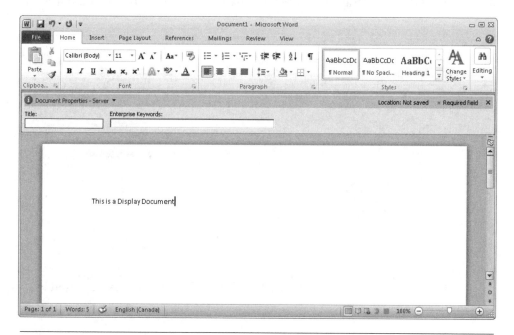

FIGURE 3-11 Creating a new SharePoint document with Microsoft Word 2010

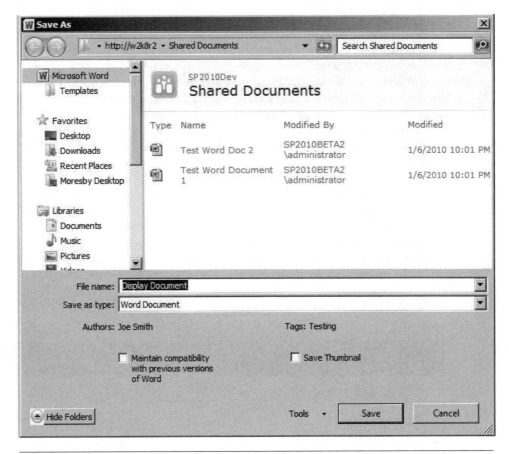

FIGURE 3-12   Saving the new document to a SharePoint library

plan because it allows you to leverage features such as versioning, workflow, and possibly, regular backups as well.

After covering techniques for getting files into your SharePoint server, you're probably eager to move on to some topics about what you can do with your content. With that in mind, the next section introduces some common document management tasks.

Document Tasks

Once you have your documents inside SharePoint, you'll clearly want to leverage the full potential of SharePoint document management. In this section, some of the most common document tasks are discussed.

Deleting a Document

After covering the subject of adding to SharePoint, it seems only natural to move on to removing documents from SharePoint. Although SharePoint does have a Recycle Bin, content in the bin will expire over time, so before you trash something, make sure that you really don't need it. After something has been completely removed from SharePoint, the only way to recover it is to get it from a database backup. Without a third-party restore tool, this can literally take an entire day since it involves creating a new SharePoint server and then restoring the entire database—basically, not a fun day for the SharePoint administrator.

To delete a document, you can select its row by clicking on an area of the row that does not contain a link—if you were to click on one of the fields that contains a link, you would simply open that link instead of selecting the row. If you want to delete more than one document, you can select them by checking their boxes in the documents list and then choosing Delete from the ribbon.

Another way to delete a document is to choose Delete from the drop-down menu that appears when you click the down arrow next to the document's name (see Figure 3-13).

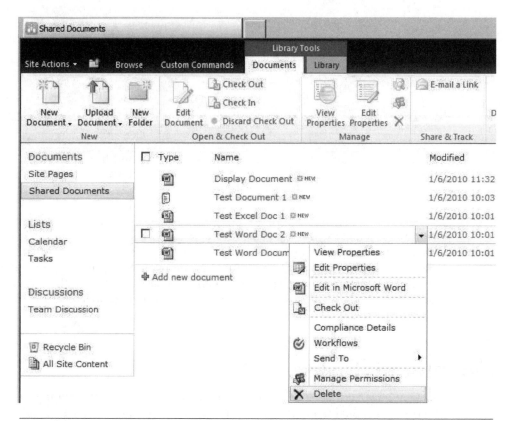

FIGURE 3-13 Selecting the option to delete a document from the list

As you would expect, SharePoint then asks you to confirm the delete action via a dialog. You'll need to confirm that you do, in fact, want to delete the selected items from the list. After you confirm the delete action, you may see an indicator on the far right of the screen that SharePoint is removing the selected files.

 Tip You can also delete an item by selecting it and then pressing the DELETE key. Many more SharePoint keyboard shortcuts are available, but at the time of writing, the list of SharePoint 2010 hot keys has not been published.

When the document has been removed, it may not be completely purged from the SharePoint server—it will usually end up in the site's Recycle Bin. This leads into the next topic. What if you want to recover a document that you or someone else has deleted?

Recovering a Document from the Recycle Bin

If you discover that you or someone else has deleted a file that you need to return to SharePoint, you should first check the Recycle Bin. If you check before the content expires, you'll be able to easily restore the file.

To check the Recycle Bin, navigate to the site that contained the deleted document and simply look at the bottom of the left-hand navigation pane for the Recycle Bin link. Click this link and the site's Recycle Bin will open (see Figure 3-14).

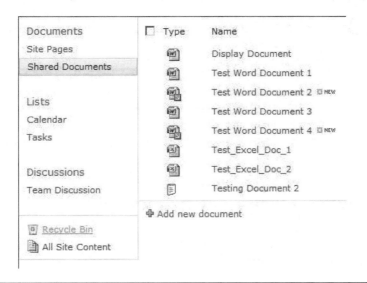

FIGURE 3-14   The link to the Recycle Bin is on many pages.

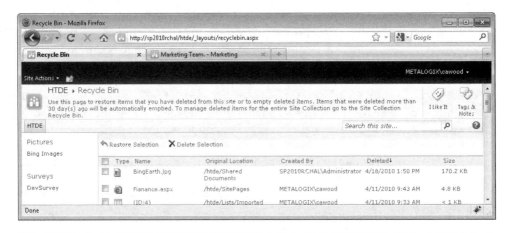

FIGURE 3-15 The SharePoint Recycle Bin

Once you have navigated to the site's Recycle Bin, you'll see a list of all the content that can be restored. Click the check box next to each item you need to restore, and then click Restore Selection (see Figure 3-15).

A dialog pops up and asks if you're really truly sure that you want to restore the selected content.

The Recycle Bin is certainly a useful tool in SharePoint. However, it should be considered a last resort. Try to avoid making use of it on a regular basis.

 SharePoint actually has a two-stage Recycle Bin system. If you cannot find your file, ask your administrator to check the other Recycle Bin. Neither of the bins is permanent, so eventually, deleted items will be removed from the SharePoint database. The first stage, the site Recycle Bin, can be set to expire after a certain number of days (30 days is the default setting). The second stage, the site collection Recycle Bin, can be set to expire when it reaches a certain storage capacity (50% is the default setting). So, by default, deleted items stay in the site Recycle Bin for 30 days and then move to the site collection Recycle Bin, from which the administrator can still recover the items (subject to sufficient storage capacity). You can think of the second stage as the "global" Recycle Bin.

Viewing Document Properties

You'll often need to check into the finer details of your documents. This information is stored in the document's metadata. Naturally, SharePoint documents contain a great deal of metadata information, and getting familiar with what's available and where to find it will make things easier for you.

The quickest way to look for metadata is to access the default document properties. What you'll find there will vary slightly, but information such as Name and Title is common. To see the properties of your documents, select a document from within

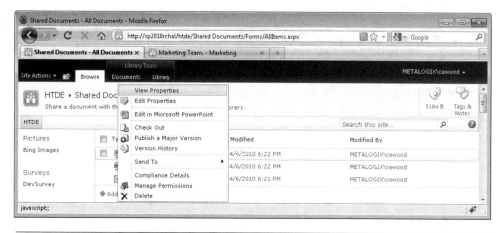

FIGURE 3-16   Choosing to view the properties of a document

a document library, click its drop-down arrow, and choose View Properties (see Figure 3-16). If you prefer, you can also use the View Properties option in the ribbon.

After you make your selection, the properties dialog opens, enabling you to see the properties of the document (see Figure 3-17).

Viewing properties is one thing, but if you have sufficient permissions, you'll also be able to make changes.

Editing Document Properties

There are countless reasons why you might want to change the metadata associated with documents in SharePoint. For example, maybe the filenames used during the

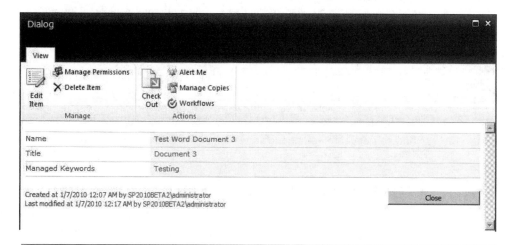

FIGURE 3-17   Viewing the properties of a document

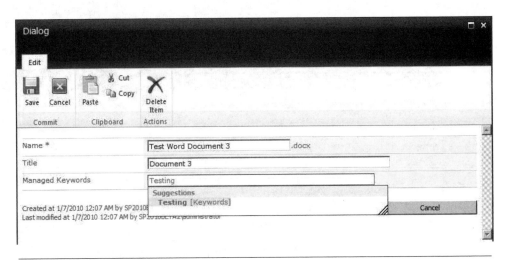

FIGURE 3-18 Editing a document's properties

upload were the cryptic filename values from the file system and now you want to make use of SharePoint's potential by assigning user-friendly titles.

As you did in the previous example, the first step is to find your document. Then, either use the Edit Properties button on the ribbon, or click the document's drop-down arrow and select the Edit Properties command.

When the dialog opens, you'll be able to alter any properties that you have rights to edit (see Figure 3-18).

 You will not be able to see every metadata value in the property edit dialog. You can think of each column of data in a list as a different metadata value. Not all of the columns are shown in the default list view, and they certainly aren't all shown in the property edit dialog. If you are looking for information that does not show by default, you may need to create your own custom view. Creating your own list views is discussed in Chapter 9.

 With the new Enterprise Metadata Management (EMM) functionality in SharePoint 2010, it's possible that you'll need to frequently edit document properties to tag them with taxonomy metadata. The information you add may seem unrelated to your daily tasks, but it will empower a number of use cases on your SharePoint server. For example, adding extra metadata will improve searches so that you can find content throughout the server. SharePoint taxonomy is discussed in Chapter 5.

Using Document Versioning

Now that you have an understanding of how easy it is to add, remove, open, or edit a document in SharePoint, it's time to talk about version control. Versioning is not required on document libraries, but it's a useful feature and widely used. Versioning gives you the ability to create a new copy—minor or major—of a document each time you make an edit. Of course, you wouldn't want two people working on the same version of the document at the same time, so you also need another important SharePoint document management feature, workflow.

The simplest workflow in SharePoint is the content approval workflow that's included in the document library versioning settings: requiring that a user check out a document before that user can make a change. If another user wants to edit the same document, he or she will have to wait until the document is checked in before he or she can check it out and make changes. Before delving into the details of versioning, here are some basic content approval examples.

Checking Out Documents

If a document library has been configured to require check-out before making changes, then you'll need to click the document's drop-down arrow and select Check Out before you'll be allowed to open it for editing (see Figure 3-19).

Of course, as with so many options, you can also check out a document using the ribbon. You'll find the Check Out option under the Documents tab (see Figure 3-20).

After you choose Check Out, SharePoint opens a dialog that asks whether you'd like to copy the file into your local drafts folder. If you choose Yes, you'll be able to disconnect from the SharePoint server (for example, to take your laptop home) and work on the document offline. Once you are finished with your edits, you can

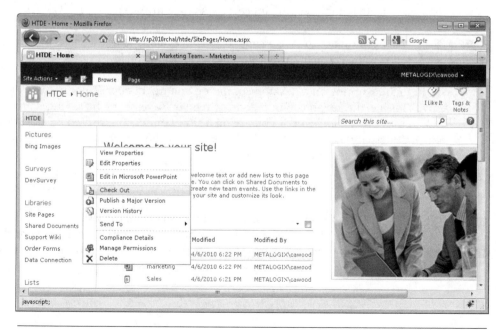

FIGURE 3-19   Selecting Check Out in a document library

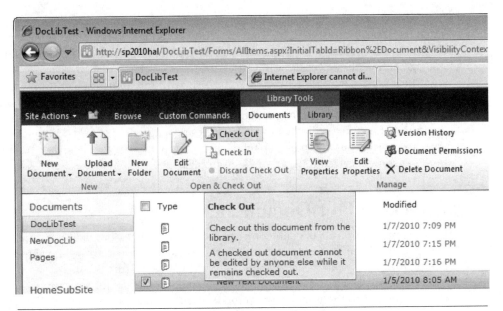

FIGURE 3-20 Using the ribbon to check out a document

reconnect to the server and save your document back into its document library. If you choose not to copy a local version, you'll only be able to save your changes while you're connected to the SharePoint server (see Figure 3-21).

 When you choose to save a copy to your local drafts folder, a SharePoint Drafts folder will be created in your Documents folder in Windows.

If you're working on a desktop computer, you might choose not to save a local copy. This has the advantage in that any time you save, you'll be saving your work back to the server. However, if you are on a slow connection, this could slow down your productivity. Regardless of which option you choose, you simply need to remember to save your changes back to the server when you're done.

SharePoint will change the icon next to the document after it has been checked out—a little green arrow will be added to show that file has been checked out.

 If you choose to edit your document in the default editor assigned to the document type (for example, Microsoft Word), you will still be prompted to check out the file if check-out is required for that document library. Once the document is checked out, you will be able to edit and save your changes.

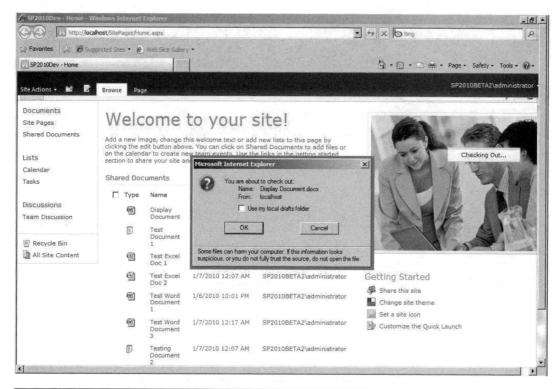

FIGURE 3-21   Confirming document check-out

Checking In a Document

Naturally, the topic to cover after checking out a document is how to check in a document. In addition to the usual drop-down menu and ribbon options previously discussed, if you're using Microsoft Office clients, there's also a way to check in from the client.

Checking In with SharePoint

The first technique is to simply go to the library and use the drop-down menu or the ribbon. You might expect that SharePoint would simply check in the document

---

Did You Know?

Check Out from the Document Properties Dialog

It's worth mentioning that it's also possible to check out a document from the document properties dialog (see Figure 3-22). You may not use this feature, but just keep in mind that it's there.

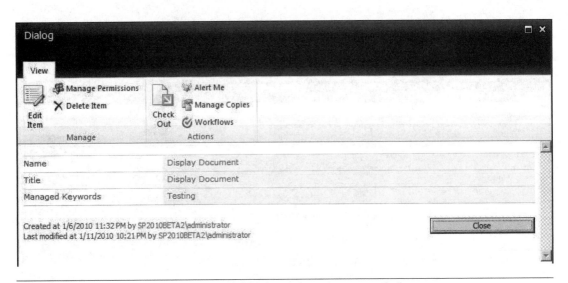

FIGURE 3-22 Check Out is also available from the properties dialog.

and you'd be done, but that's not the case. When you check in, SharePoint asks if you want to retain the check-out status after the document has been checked in (see Figure 3-23).

This option may seem counterintuitive at first, but there is a logical reason for it. If you were working on a document and wanted to check it in to create a version, but you didn't want anyone altering the document before you make further changes, then you could retain the check-out and not risk the chance that another user would check out the document before you remembered to check it out again.

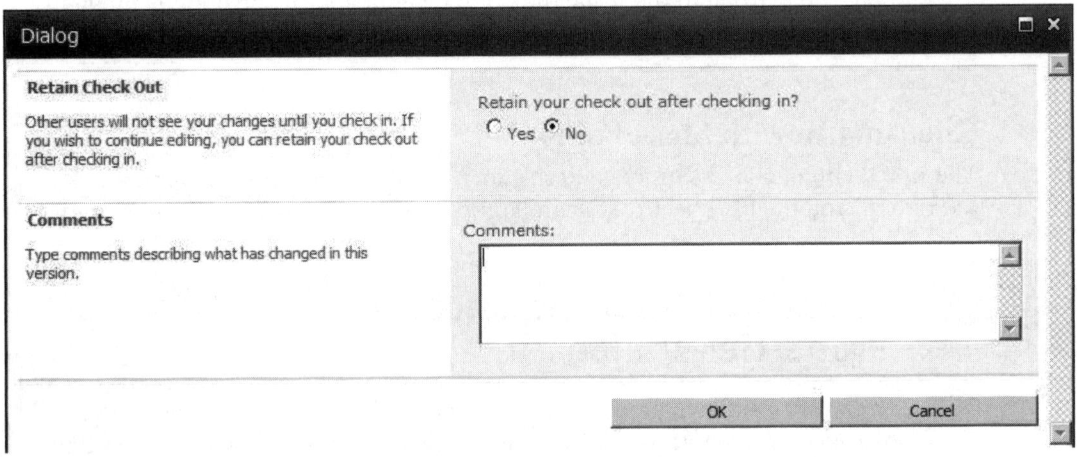

FIGURE 3-23 Retain Check Out dialog

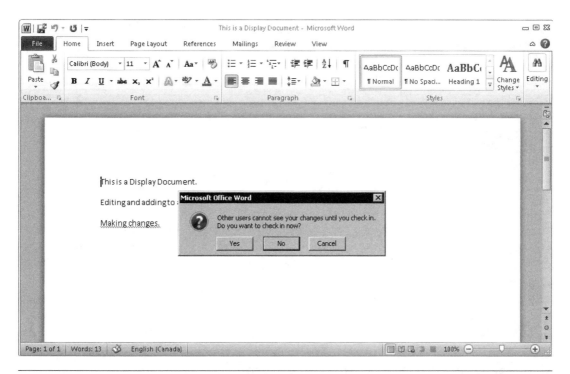

FIGURE 3-24 Check in from Microsoft Word 2010

In this dialog, you'll also be asked for a check-in comment. In the default content approval process, this comment is optional, but it can be very useful when you're looking through old versions of files and trying to figure out why a certain change was made.

Checking In with Microsoft Word

Another way to check in a SharePoint file is from one of the many clients that support SharePoint content approval workflow. If you're editing a file in Word, when you save and close the file, the client will ask if you want to check in (see Figure 3-24).

If you want to check in a file from a client without closing the document, you can also choose File | Info and then choose to check in from the available options (see Figure 3-25).

Note The interface used for this example is part of the new Microsoft Office 2010 Fluent Backstage view. Backstage offers a tighter integration between SharePoint and Microsoft applications, including Access 2010, Excel 2010, InfoPath 2010, OneNote 2010, PowerPoint 2010, Project 2010, Publisher 2010, SharePoint Designer 2010, Visio 2010, and Word 2010.

FIGURE 3-25 Check in from the Microsoft Word 2010 File menu

As with the other techniques, the client program will ask you to enter a check-in comment (see Figure 3-26).

The client Info page shows all sorts of interesting information about SharePoint files. You'll be able to see properties of the document, as well as information about versions, permissions, and more.

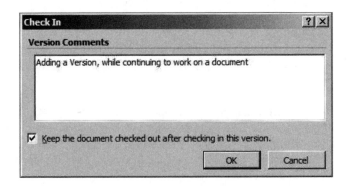

FIGURE 3-26 Adding a check-in comment from Microsoft Word

Approving a Document for Publishing

The subject of SharePoint workflow could easily fill a couple of books on its own. Topics include the default built-in content approval workflow associated with various list templates, designing workflows with the visual workflow designer, designing custom workflows in SharePoint Designer, and even developing custom workflows in Visual Studio. For the purposes of this book, only the built-in SharePoint content approval workflow functionality will be discussed. This section provides just a few key examples.

Content approval requires that an item be approved before it is published in SharePoint. In fact, this simple type of workflow is so commonplace that there is an option to enable it in the library settings of document libraries. Once the option has been enabled, any document that is checked in will have to be approved before the changes are available. To approve or reject the changes, a user with approval rights needs to select the Approve/Reject option from the drop-down menu (see Figure 3-27) or the ribbon.

You probably noted already that the option Approve/Reject implies that there's more to this option than just approving an edit. In addition to the ability to approve any edits since the last approval, you also have the option to reject the changes

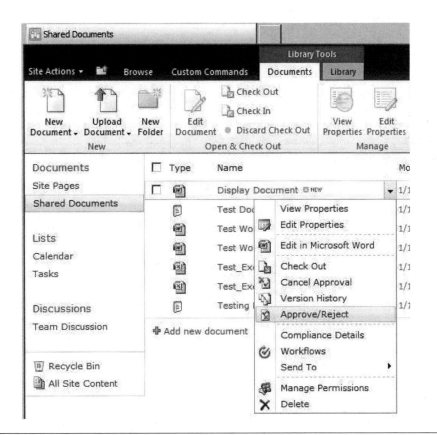

FIGURE 3-27   The Approve/Reject drop-down menu option

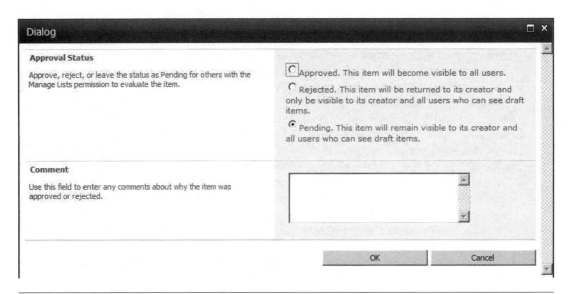

FIGURE 3-28 The approval dialog

(see Figure 3-28). In addition, there is a Comment text box that allows you to enter a comment that explains your choice or adds information for anyone who might be interested in the history of the document.

After you have selected the appropriate option, you'll be returned to the document library and the change will be shown in the Approval Status column.

 The Approval Status column only appears if the library has been set to require approval.

Having covered the straightforward options in basic content approval workflow, the next topics delve a little deeper into the document version options. For example, what if versioning isn't enabled on a library, or what if you needed to find previous versions of a document?

More About Versions

There are many reasons to take advantage of the document versioning features available in SharePoint. This section covers some more aspects of versioning that you'll find useful if you choose to take advantage of this functionality.

Turning On Versioning

Suppose that your organization is legally required to keep all versions of documents. To make what might seem like a cumbersome task easy to enforce, simply enable SharePoint version control.

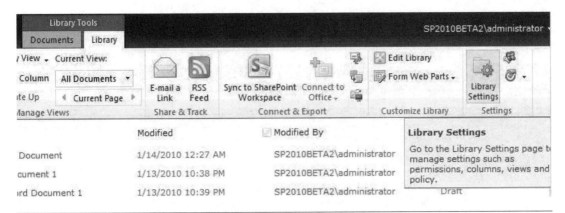

FIGURE 3-29   The library settings are accessible from the ribbon

To turn on versioning in a document library, click the Library tab on the ribbon and then click Library Settings (see Figure 3-29).

There are many options within the Document Library Settings page. Versioning Settings is the second link down in the General Settings section (see Figure 3-30).

 Any Settings page in SharePoint has a URL, so just like any other page, you can bookmark a Settings page for easy access in the future.

On the Document Library Versioning Settings page, you have a number of options (see Figure 3-31). The settings are divided into the following sections:

- **Content Approval**   Here you can specify whether approval is required for items in the library. This is an example of using a simple out-of-the-box SharePoint workflow feature.
- **Document Version History**   This section gives you options for how versions will be created. If you want, you can disable versioning, create just major versions, or create major versions and minor versions. In addition, you have the option to specify how many versions of the document SharePoint will retain. If storage is more important than retaining every copy of your documents, you may choose to limit the number of versions SharePoint keeps in its database. The decision of whether to create minor (draft) versions is more subtle; there may be many cases where the difference isn't important to you. However, if you want to be able to create multiple draft versions and then only "publish" by creating a major version, then you'll need to have both types of versions available.
- **Draft Item Security**   This option allows you to restrict access to minor versions. As you would expect, this option is only available if both minor and major versions are enabled.
- **Require Check Out**   This is another handy built-in workflow feature. If you want to enforce that only one person can be working on an item at a time, you can require users to check out the document before editing.

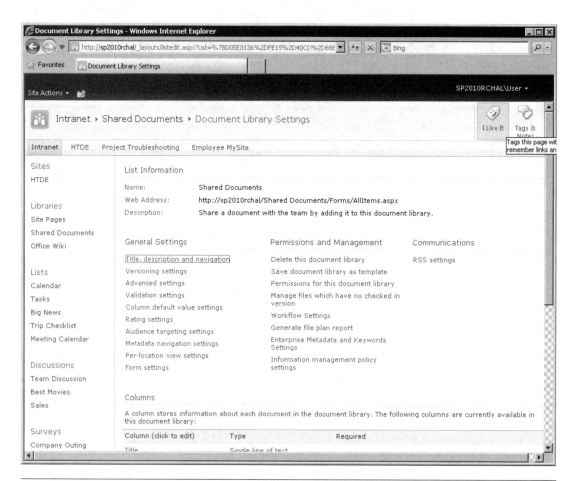

FIGURE 3-30 The Document Library Settings page

 The number of versions you decide to keep will be N+1. For example, if you chose to keep five versions, there could be six copies of a document in the library. The current "master" copy and five historical versions of it.

Working with Version History

Naturally, versions are only useful if you have an easy way to access the metadata for your versions, view old versions, and—in the worst case—restore an old version over the top of the current version. To see a list of the versions of a particular document that SharePoint has stored, select a document and choose the Version History option in the actions drop-down menu.

The version history dialog will open and show the versions that are stored in SharePoint (see Figure 3-32). This dialog shows both minor and major versions, as

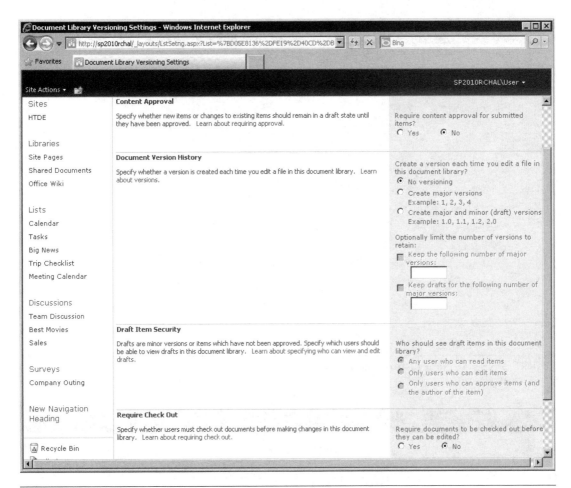

FIGURE 3-31 The version settings page for a document library

well as the modified date, who modified the version, the size of the particular version of the file, and any version comments that have been added.

If you click the date field in the Modified column, a drop-down menu appears with the options to View, Restore, or Delete that version (see Figure 3-33).

Choosing to view the information about a version will open a new dialog in which you can see all the metadata about the version in question. For the default document library list template, this includes the name, title, managed keywords, and approval status. In addition to this, you'll also see information that will be helpful if you need to figure out which version contains some information that you need to view again. This includes the version numbers, the created date, and the last modified date—the latter two also include the user information for that data.

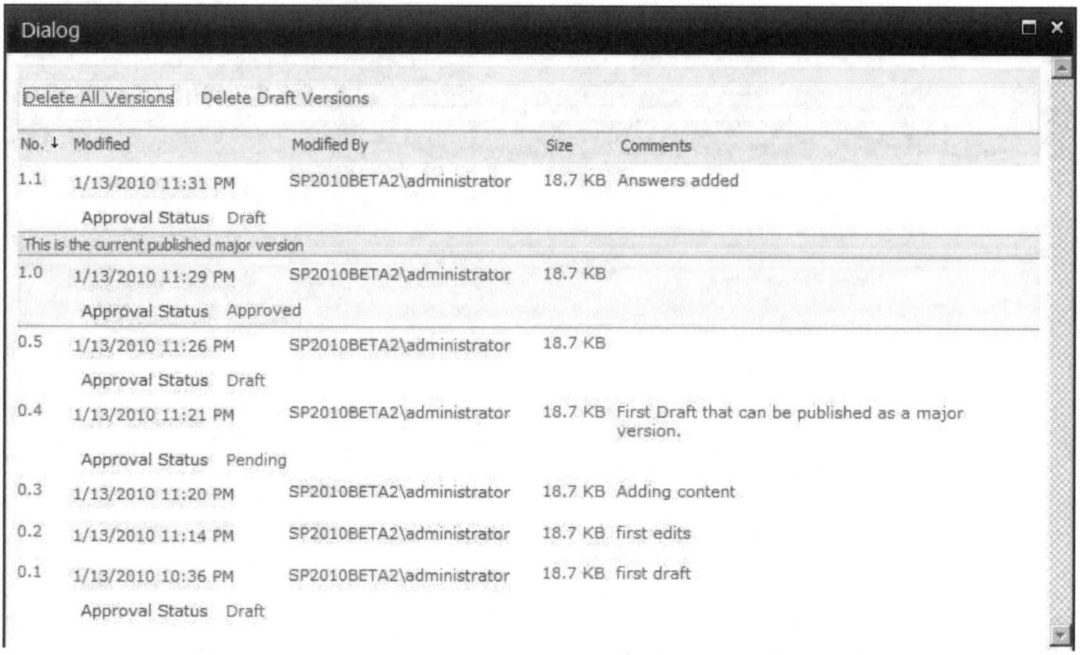

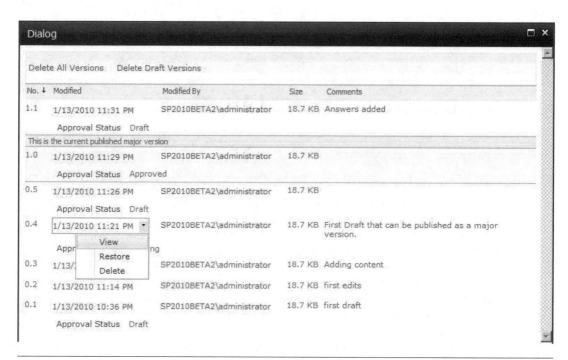

FIGURE 3-32 Version history dialog

FIGURE 3-33 Version dialog drop-down menu

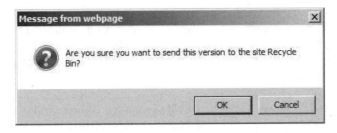

FIGURE 3-34   Deleting a document version

If you choose to delete a version, you will be prompted to confirm the operation (see Figure 3-34). One reason you might delete old versions is to save space.

   The default of infinite versions could lead to a full server, quickly. For example a 5MB Word document saved 20 times will use 100MB of storage for a single document. If you suspect that you'll have to perform some housecleaning on a document library because of storage considerations, you might want to set a maximum number of versions in the library settings. Just remember that—after some time—there will be no way to easily recover the versions that are removed as a result of the policy you set.

Restoring a version is just as easy as deleting one. When you choose Restore in the drop-down menu, the dialog shown in Figure 3-35 appears. Restore could be

FIGURE 3-35   Restoring a version

particularly useful in cases where versioning has been enabled on a library, but approval is not required. If a team is collaborating on items in such a library, one user may make a change that isn't acceptable to another user. Since no approval was required when the item was checked in, the best way to undo the edits might be to restore one of the older versions.

 Restore makes the selected old version the current version. This means that the current version will get stored as an older version in the history. In other words, if you restore a version, you are putting it "in front of" the most recent version, thus demoting that newer version to an older version.

Summary

This chapter should have provided you with enough information to start working efficiently with SharePoint documents. Whether you need to add documents, use the SharePoint content approval workflow, or work with document versions, the topics covered will help you quickly navigate the various options and choose what will work best for you and/or your team.

4

Collaboration

As the name "SharePoint" implies, collaboration has been at the core of SharePoint's functionality since its very conception. However, a great deal has happened in the domain of social networking since the release of SharePoint Portal Server 2001. The ever increasing popularity of tools such as blogs and wikis has significantly improved the way people collaborate.

In this chapter, we'll take a look at the various ways that SharePoint Server 2010 can grease the wheels of collaboration. Some of the topics in this chapter also fit into other chapters, but they're covered together here for your convenience.

Discussion Boards

When talking about collaboration, back-and-forth conversation is the logical starting place. SharePoint provides discussion board lists exactly for this purpose.

Back in 1980, a discussion board system called Usenet was launched. Usenet eventually became the world's most popular discussion system, and it retained that status until Internet forum sites came along to displace it as the most prominent technology for online discussions. Although the ability to access Usenet groups through a web browser makes them no more difficult to use than other types of Internet forums, Usenet's centralized system has been supplanted by the multitude of decentralized forums that have been spawned over the last 15 years. The main reason is that systems such as SharePoint discussion boards can provide both the usability of other technologies and the option to maintain complete control over data and security.

In this section, you'll learn how to create and use SharePoint discussion boards to enable conversations among your users.

Creating a New Discussion Board

As with most lists, the first thing you do when you want to create a discussion board is expand the Site Actions drop-down menu and choose More Options (see Figure 4-1). This opens the Create dialog and allows you to choose what you would like to create.

There are other ways to create a list. For example, you could choose the View All Site Content menu item under Site Actions and then click the Create link (see Figure 4-2).

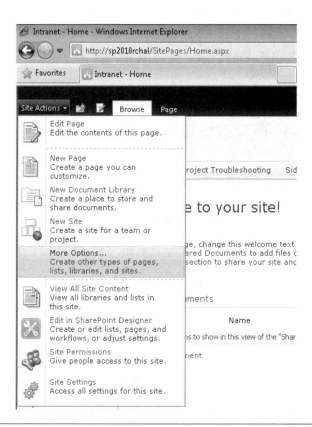

FIGURE 4-1   More Options from the Site Actions menu

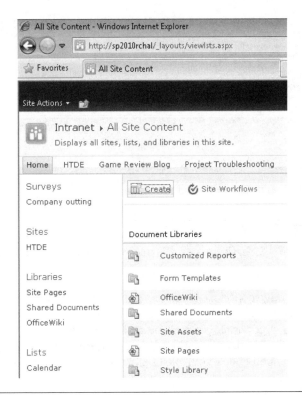

FIGURE 4-2   The Create link under the View All Site Content option

Once you have the Create dialog open, you simply choose the category on the left and then select the type of library, list, page, or site that you'd like to create on the right. In this case, choose to filter by the List type and then click the Discussion Board icon (see Figure 4-3). To finish creating the board, you just need to fill in the Name field on the right and click the Create button.

If you would like to give your discussion board a description or change the setting that determines if the board will appear in the quick launch for your site, click the More Options button before you create the board.

Now that you have created a discussion board, you can begin to create discussion threads and invite people to join into the conversation.

Using a Discussion Board

Now that you have created a new discussion board list, you'll obviously want to start using it. Conversations within discussion boards are divided into threads. Within threads you'll find the original message and any replies that have been posted.

To create a new thread, click the Add New Discussion link. This opens the New Item dialog and allows you to add the subject and body of your discussion post (see Figure 4-4).

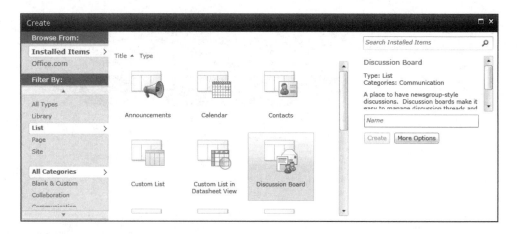

FIGURE 4-3 Creating a new discussion board from the Create dialog

In the Body section, you can use many text formatting features. If you change to the Insert tab, you'll also have the option to add tables, pictures, links, file attachments, and possibly video and audio files as well. These features are all provided to enable the richest possible experience in your discussions. Don't forget that you can spell check your post before saving it. After you save your post, it will

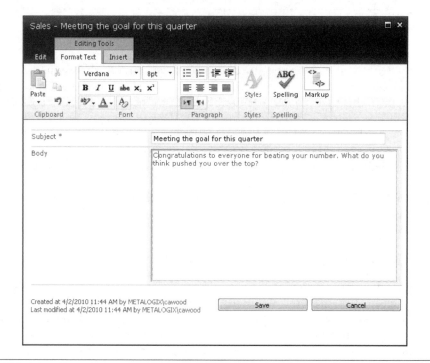

FIGURE 4-4 Creating a new thread

appear in the thread. In this example, a photo is added to the user's profile so that there is a more personal feel to SharePoint social interactions such as conversations in discussion boards. Personalizing your profile will be covered in Chapter 7.

 Note The spell check feature is not available in SharePoint Foundation 2010.

Naturally, discussions aren't very interesting unless they're more than one-sided. Replying to a discussion post is as simple as clicking the Reply link and writing a message (see Figure 4-5).

After submitting the reply, it will also appear in the discussion list (see Figure 4-6). Users who have rights to the discussion will be able to contribute by adding new replies.

If you return to the main page for the discussion board, you'll see each thread in the list view (see Figure 4-7). In the list view, you can take advantage of the standard list management features such as being able to delete multiple items in one operation.

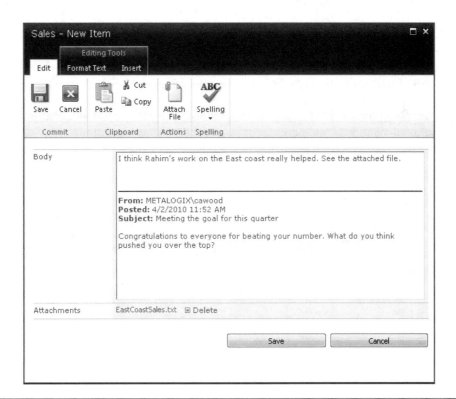

FIGURE 4-5 Replying to a thread

FIGURE 4-6 The thread view after a reply

Editing a Discussion Board Item

Although you generally won't need to take advantage of these options, it is possible to delete threads, individual posts, or the whole discussion board. Maybe an employee accidentally included sensitive information in a post, or you decided that an old thread should be deleted in favor of a brand new conversation.

FIGURE 4-7 Discussion board threads shown in list view

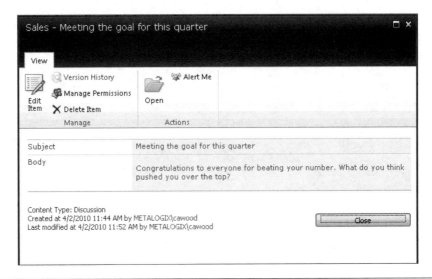

FIGURE 4-8   Viewing the properties of a discussion board post

Whatever the reason you need to manage the discussion posts, viewing and editing a post is easy. To open the properties view, simply click the View Properties option next to the post. Once there, you'll also have options to edit the item (see Figure 4-8).

 Just like other lists, discussion boards can be set up to require approval, so if you're really worried about what information might be getting out, you can turn it on.

Using Discussion Boards from Microsoft Outlook

If you are using Microsoft Outlook as your e-mail client, you have the option of connecting to SharePoint from Outlook. One such use case is discussion boards. Users can reply and carry on conversations in a SharePoint discussion board from within the Outlook interface.

To open the discussion board in Outlook, choose the Connect to Outlook option from the ribbon. When you select this option, you need to accept a couple of security validations. These safeguards prevent malware programs from connecting to SharePoint. In this case, you're authorizing Outlook to read and write to your SharePoint discussion board.

After connecting your discussion board, you can open Outlook and the list will appear in the SharePoint Lists section of the left navigation pane in the Outlook client (see Figure 4-9). You can then read and respond to discussion board posts directly from Outlook.

Accessing SharePoint content from Outlook can often help with SharePoint adoption for users who are hooked on e-mail. In the discussion board case, they will be able to discuss in Outlook as they would in e-mail, but the content is stored in SharePoint, which means that it's available and searchable through the standard SharePoint interfaces.

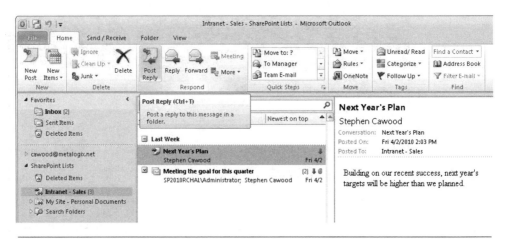

FIGURE 4-9 A discussion board open in Outlook 2010

Alerts

If you would like to keep up to date on what's happening on your SharePoint server, alerts are a great tool. Adding an alert is as simple as going to the List or Library tab and choosing to set an alert. For example, to receive an e-mail notification when someone replies to a thread on a discussion board, you can add an alert (see Figure 4-10).

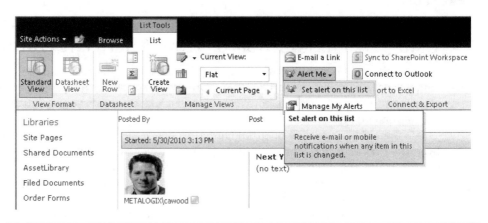

FIGURE 4-10 Adding an alert to a discussion board

Blogs

Discussion boards may be the best answer to your two-way conversation needs, but there's no doubt that web logs, known as blogs, are the way to publish and share your writing. Many companies have started to use internal blogs as part of their knowledge management system. For example, a blog can be used to create a knowledge base for frequently asked questions (FAQs). If an employee leaves, her blog remains and the company doesn't completely lose the value of that employee.

According to blog search engine Technorati, there are over 112,000,000 web logs already on the Internet and more are being added each day. Blogs are everywhere, whether they post gadget reviews, such as www.gizmodo.com, or humorous stories, such as www.wiihaveaproblem.com, which records tales about damage caused while people play the Wii video game console.

In SharePoint Server 2010, blogs are a type of site template. As you've already seen, there are a few methods to create sites such as blogs. One option is to go to Site Actions | More Options.

Once you've created your new blog site, you'll see that the first post is created for you (see Figure 4-11). Of course, you can choose to delete this welcome post, but there is no need to do so; you could also simply modify it if you want.

 You can also add a blog to your My Sites. My Sites are discussed in more detail in Chapter 7.

FIGURE 4-11 A new blog site

To begin posting to your blog, choose the Create a Post link on the right side of the page. The blog authoring dialog is similar to the dialog that you've already seen for discussion boards. However, the blog dialog also gives you the option of adding categories to your posts (see Figure 4-12). Similar to other taxonomy features in SharePoint, these categories allow your readers to filter your blog for the posts that apply to certain topics. You can use the Add New Category link on the left side of the blog site to add new topics to the list.

When a blog is created, three blog categories are created out of the box. There are a few ways to change the names of these categories. The simplest method is to click the Categories title, switch to Datasheet View, and overwrite each name.

Look for the RSS link to get the URL for your blog feed. The feed allows others to be notified when a new post has been added. You can add RSS feeds to your browser and to applications such as Microsoft Outlook.

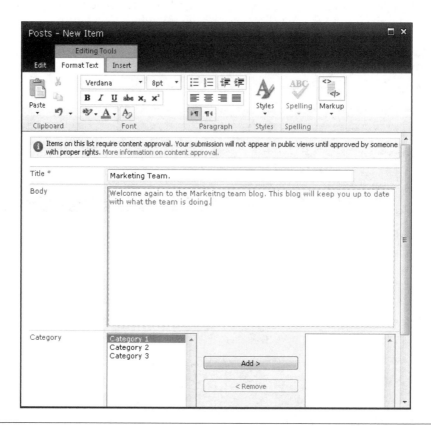

FIGURE 4-12 Authoring a new blog post using the SharePoint web interface

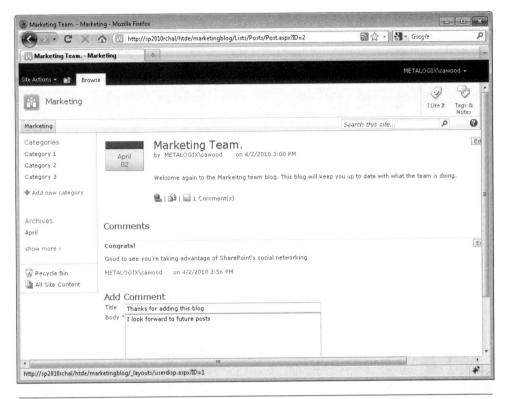

FIGURE 4-13   Adding a blog comment

Posting Blog Comments

Blogs may not be as interactive as a discussion board, but that doesn't mean that they are only one-way. If you want to share your thoughts on someone's blog posts, you'll be able to post a blog comment (see Figure 4-13).

On the main blog page, you'll see a summary of the most recent posts. At the bottom of each post, you'll see a link to the comments and also a "permalink," or permanent link, which is a direct link to that post. After other posts have been added, the postings in the summary view will eventually change, but the permalink will always point directly to the posting, so if you want someone to read a particular post, you should send that URL to them.

Managing Blog Posts

When viewing a blog site—as a user with sufficient privileges, of course—you will notice that there is an Edit link next to each post. Clicking this link allows you to make changes to the post. If, for example, you notice a spelling mistake or other typo, you can use the edit option to quickly correct the mistake.

FIGURE 4-14 Managing blog posts

However, if you'd like to work with the blog items in the usual SharePoint list view (see Figure 4-14), you can click the Manage Posts link.

If you'd like to use Microsoft Word to write your blog posts, just click the Launch Blog Program to Post link (under Blog Tools) on the blog page. Some people prefer to blog in Microsoft Word because they can take advantage of unique Word features such as SmartArt.

Blogging with Windows Live Writer

If you're a fan of Windows client applications, you may not want to use the SharePoint web interface to record your deepest thoughts in your SharePoint blogs. You may also want to have a WYSIWYG editor that allows you to work offline. If either of these things appeals to you, you should try Microsoft Windows Live Writer (http://download.live.com/writer) for blogging (see Figure 4-15).

Since Live Writer is a free application, you can download it and try it quite easily. Once you have the application installed, you can go into Tools | Accounts and add your blog accounts (see Figure 4-16). Many of the most popular blogging applications—including SharePoint, of course—are supported. While you're in there, you might wish to check out some of the other options.

One of the options provided is to automatically upload to an FTP server any images you drag and drop (or paste) into your posts. This is useful if you're already using an FTP server to store files for you.

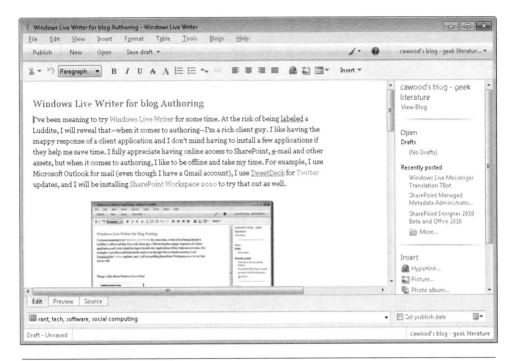

FIGURE 4-15   Windows Live Writer

To start writing, choose File | New Post and start writing. One of the benefits of using a Windows client program for blog authoring is that you can easily add images wherever you want them and size them to match your needs—and you can do all of this without having to know anything about the underlying HTML code. Simply drag and drop or copy and paste to add an image, and then use the mouse to size the picture as needed.

The blog page is actually a web part page, so if you switch to edit mode, you'll be able to add web parts.

Now, instead of waiting until your flight lands, you'll be able to blog away at 30,000 feet.

At the time of writing, Windows Live Writer was still using the old Windows menu paradigm. It is likely that the next version will use the Fluent UI Ribbon interface, so the screenshots in this section may be different from what you see when you install the application.

FIGURE 4-16 Opening a SharePoint blog with Windows Live Writer

 By default, Site Owners and Approvers (Designers) are the only users who can directly publish blog posts—everyone else submits a post as a draft that needs to be approved. To change this behavior, navigate to your blog site and choose Site Actions | View All Site Content | Posts | List Settings | Versioning Settings. In the Content Approval settings, the first option is Require Content Approval for Submitted Items. If you turn off this option, no one will need their posts to be approved.

Wikis

If you've ever used Wikipedia.com, then you've benefited from the potential of wiki sites. The name wiki comes from the Hawaiian word for quick. The creators of the wiki realized that the best way to create a lasting and shared store of knowledge was to make contributing and editing quick and easy.

In SharePoint Server 2010 there are a couple of options for creating wikis. One is the wiki page library and the other is the enterprise wiki site template. The wiki page library is closer to what most people would think of as a traditional wiki website.

These types of libraries are commonly used on intranets to publish web-accessible, living documents that need to be edited frequently. Enterprise wikis combine wiki functionality with other features such as project management.

In this section, you'll get an introduction to wikis, but first you'll need to create a wiki to experiment with. As you'd expect, the process for creating a wiki page library is the same as for creating other types of lists: Site Actions | More Options. After you choose the wiki page library, SharePoint will create the library and fill in the first page with some welcome content—just like you saw when you created a blog in the previous section.

Of course, the benefit of a wiki is collaborative editing. Unless you and your fellow SharePoint users are making edits, there won't be much combined value to your wikis. To start editing, click the Edit tab at the top of the page and then click the Edit button. Many users choose to remove the sample content as their first edit.

One of the ease-of-use features built into wiki libraries is shorthand syntax for adding links and creating new wiki pages. The syntax for a link is "[[*Link Text*]]." While in edit mode, simply type **[[** and you'll be offered a choice of pages to link to (see Figure 4-17).

 This functionality works on any SharePoint dashboard page.

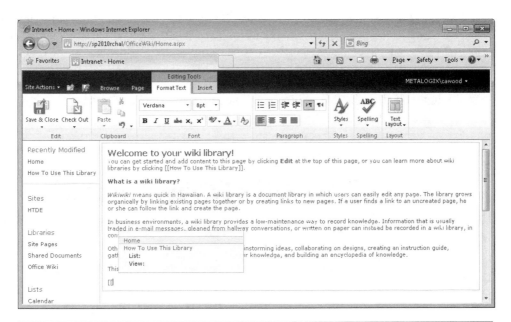

FIGURE 4-17   Adding a new link to a wiki page

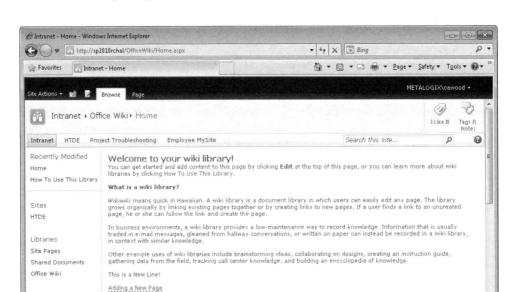

FIGURE 4-18   A wiki link to a page that doesn't exist yet

To create a new wiki page, create a link the same way that you would for an existing page—just type the name of the page you want in square brackets. After you save the page, you'll see that the link has a dotted line below it to show that the page doesn't exist yet (see Figure 4-18).

After adding the link, all you need to do is save the page and then click the link. When you click the link, a dialog will pop up and ask you whether you'd like to create the page (see Figure 4-19).

FIGURE 4-19   The New Page dialog

After you have created your wiki, you can send out the URL to your colleagues and start working together to create content. Some content will need to be tightly controlled and may require an editorial process, but other topics can benefit from groups of users being able to quickly make changes and correct errors.

Here are some examples of how SharePoint users have been leveraging wikis:

- **FAQs**   Wikis are a fantastic technology for creating frequently asked question pages. The ease of team editing allows them to also be frequently updated with the most recent information.
- **Checklists**   Document a particular process that has a tendency to change and could be updated by multiple people.
- **Contacts**   If you share a detailed contact list with a group, a wiki can be a great way to manage the content.
- **Reference**   When most people think of a wiki, Wikipedia.com comes to mind. Wikipedia is an encyclopedia and an excellent demonstration of one way to use a wiki.
- **Event planning**   If you're working with a group to plan an event, then a wiki can help make collaboration easier.
- **Notes**   If you're looking for a way to quickly store information that you can access from a browser, then maybe a wiki can help.

Announcements

If you've been asked to get the word out about the company picnic or notify people about a new press release, one way to go would be to e-mail everyone who is interested. However, what if you don't know exactly who would be interested? In that case, it's probably best not to spam your entire company, but rather let people check your SharePoint site for news on the topic.

If you would like to notify your colleagues of news, one way to do it in SharePoint is to post an announcement. The announcement can not only let your colleagues know about something interesting that has happened, or is about to happen, but also provide links or other helpful information for your fellow SharePoint users.

To add a new announcement, click the Add New Announcement link and complete the New Item dialog (see Figure 4-20).

Tip   Announcement lists can be e-mail enabled. However, e-mail–enabled lists need to be configured by a SharePoint administrator. If you are able to use them, instead of going to the SharePoint UI, you can simply e-mail the announcement list; the subject line and body will become the announcement.

Since announcements are all about news, you can choose to have your announcements automatically disappear when they become stale. To do this, choose an expiry date for your announcements in the Expires field (see Figure 4-21). For

FIGURE 4-20 Adding a new announcement

example, suppose you want to advertise that there will be cake for Sue's birthday on Friday. You could set the announcement to expire on Saturday so that it drops off the radar once the event has passed.

 You can set the expiry date when you create the item, or you can retroactively edit the announcements item and add an expiry date later.

 As you'll see in Chapter 8, you can also create announcements in an Announcements web part.

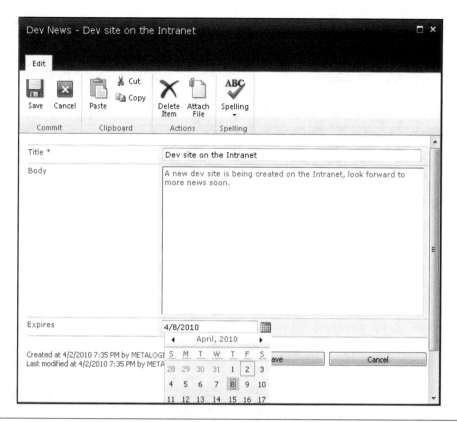

FIGURE 4-21   Setting an expiry date on a new announcement

Calendars

After finding out about an event via an announcement, the next thing SharePoint users will want to do is mark it on their calendars. SharePoint calendar lists are the best way to keep track of events, meetings, and other types of appointments.

Using one of the list creation options, choose to create a calendar. When the calendar is created, you'll see the option to create a new event on the left side of the Events tab on the ribbon (see Figure 4-22).

The New Item dialog allows you to specify details of the event (see Figure 4-23). Many of these details will be things that you'd expect to fill out on any calendar application. For example, location, start time, and description are pretty much standard. However, in a calendar item, you'll be able to take advantage of other SharePoint features such as linking the event to a SharePoint meeting workspace. Meeting workspaces are covered later in this chapter.

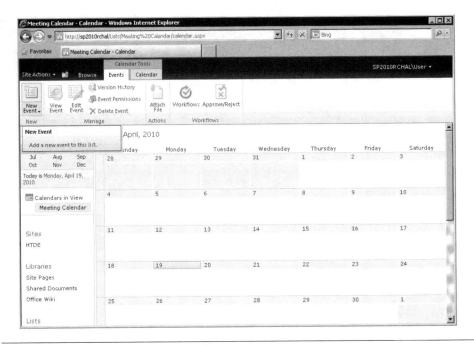

FIGURE 4-22 A SharePoint calendar

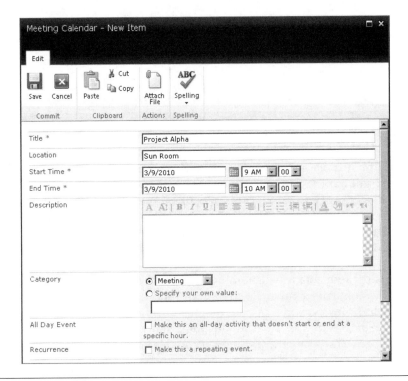

FIGURE 4-23 Adding a new event item

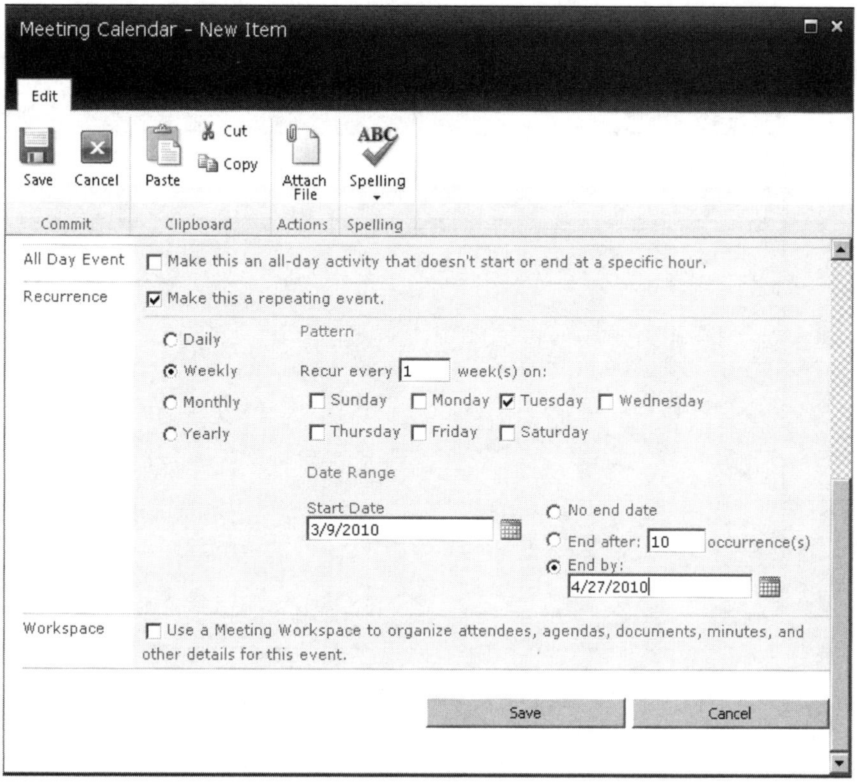

FIGURE 4-24   Setting a recurring event

An important aspect of SharePoint events is that they can be one-time or recurring. When you check the box labeled Make this a repeating event, the recurrence options will appear (see Figure 4-24). If you're familiar with Microsoft Outlook or other calendar applications, you've likely used recurring events before.

You can specify for your event to occur regularly based on time between occurrences, or you can even choose particular days or weeks to determine the recurring pattern. After you add a recurring event, you'll see that it occurs multiple times in your calendar (see Figure 4-25).

Calendar Views

Now that you've seen a few different types of lists and libraries, it's probably a good time to cover list views. Just like other lists, when you create a calendar, SharePoint will offer some different views on the list data.

However, if you would rather see the calendar in a different view, you can simply choose a different view from the Scope section of the Calendar tab on the ribbon. For example, you could switch to the Week view (see Figure 4-26). This allows you

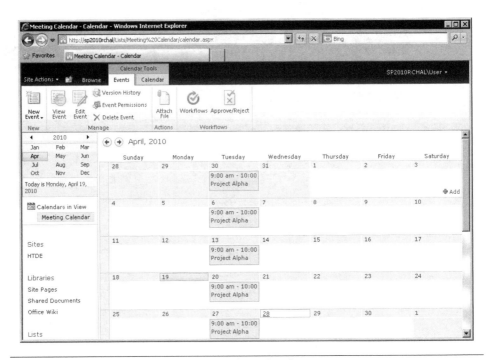

FIGURE 4-25 The recurring event in the calendar

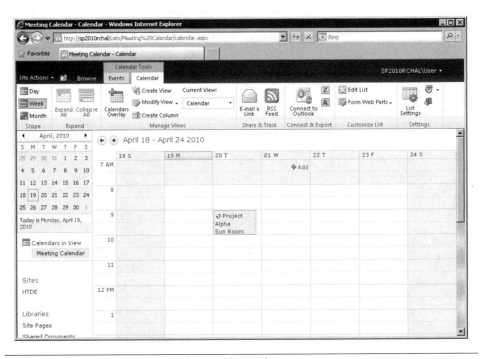

FIGURE 4-26 The same calendar in the week view

to change between the available views, but suppose that none of the existing views is able to show the list in the format you need—if you find yourself in that position, you'll want to create a custom view.

Custom Calendar Views

If you find that the out-of-the-box views either don't show the data you need to see or don't show the data in the format you need, you can create your own view. Creating a new view is not difficult. The first step is to choose the Create View option in the ribbon (see Figure 4-27).

The options on the Create View page are not just specific to calendar lists; you can use the Create View options with many SharePoint list types (see Figure 4-28).

For this example, choose the Calendar view type (see Figure 4-29). In the view options, you can choose a URL for your new view. Remember that you can bookmark the URL for easy access in the future.

If you scroll down the page, you'll see that there are even more options. For example, you can choose to filter the data to show only a subset of the calendar information. This can be useful if you find that your calendars are so full that they are difficult to read.

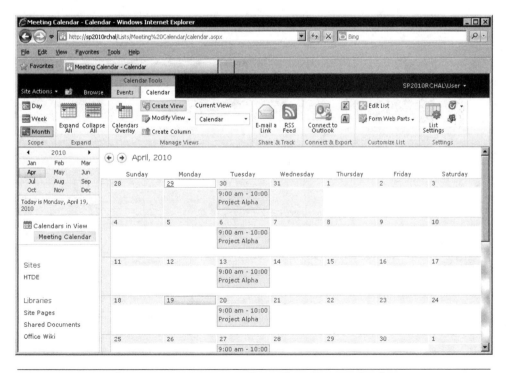

FIGURE 4-27   The Create View option for a SharePoint calendar

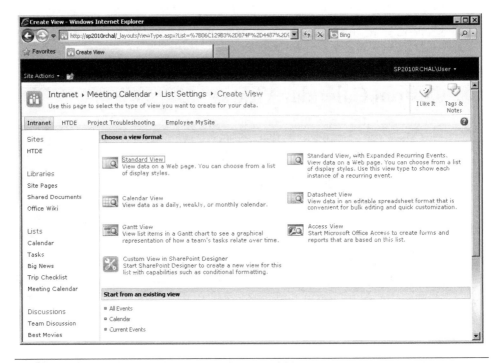

FIGURE 4-28 Create View options

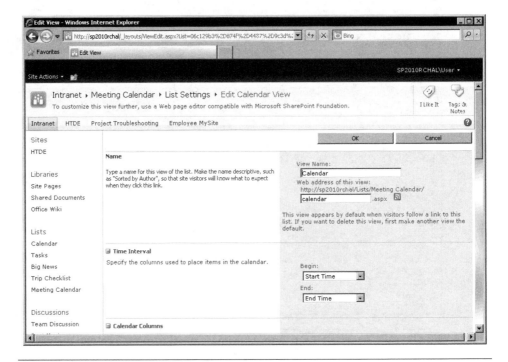

FIGURE 4-29 Calendar view options

Of course, you may not need to create a brand new view from scratch. If there is a view that's close to what you need, you might be able to modify the existing view.

 Calendars are one of the lists that can be very effectively connected to Microsoft Outlook. Refer to Chapter 10 for more information. Calendars can also be e-mail enabled.

Surveys

"How do you like SharePoint Server 2010?" "Are there enough staplers in the office?" "Are you finding this chapter useful?" These are just some of the questions you might like to ask your co-workers. Discussion boards and blog comments are one way to get feedback, but if you're looking for answers to a number of questions—and possibly anonymous responses—then a survey is the way to go. As you'd expect, the first step is to create a new list with the Survey template.

Creating a Survey

Once you have selected the Survey template, you can specify options such as whether the respondents' names will appear and whether multiple responses will be allowed from the same user (see Figure 4-30).

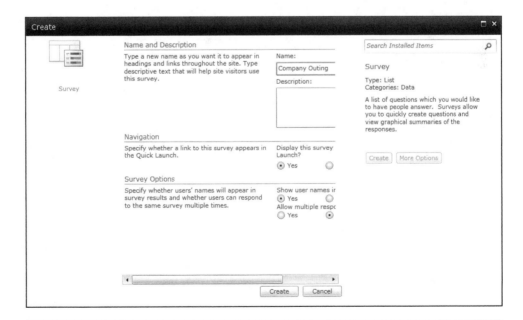

FIGURE 4-30 Survey options

After you have selected your options and SharePoint has created the list, you can start to write your questions. SharePoint allows you to pick from a wide variety of response types. These types include: Single line of text, Multiple lines of text, Choice, Rating Scale, Number, Currency, Date and Time, Lookup, Yes/No, Person or Group, External Data, and Managed Metadata (see Figure 4-31).

In this example, a Choice question type was selected, so a text box for entering the possible responses appears (see Figure 4-32).

After you have finished entering your questions, your survey item is ready to gather feedback (see Figure 4-33).

To get the news out that you have a survey ready, you might choose to send an e-mail with a link to the survey page. When someone chooses to respond, he or she will be prompted with a dialog containing the survey questions (see Figure 4-34).

Once your responses have started to roll in, you will undoubtedly want to view the results. Your options are to view a list of all the results or to see a graphical summary of the results (see Figure 4-35).

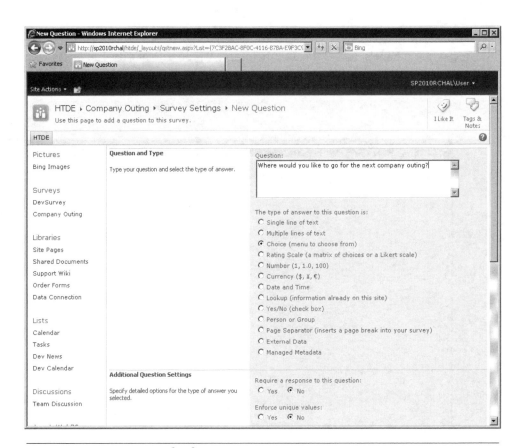

FIGURE 4-31 Creating the first survey question

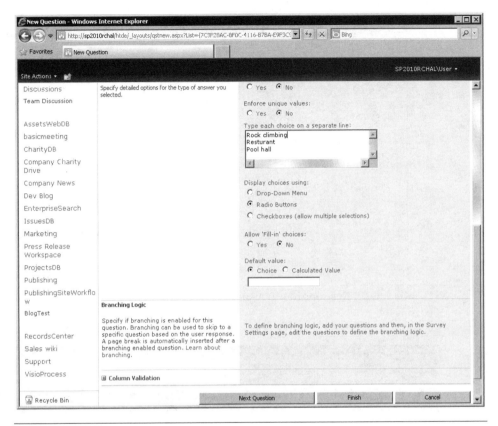

FIGURE 4-32 Specifying choices

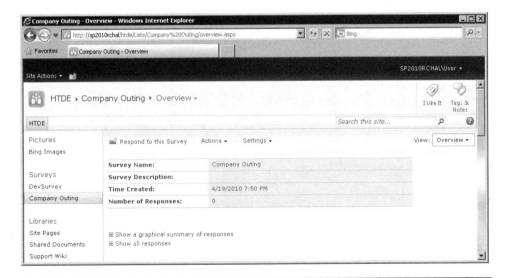

FIGURE 4-33 The survey item

FIGURE 4-34 Responding to a survey

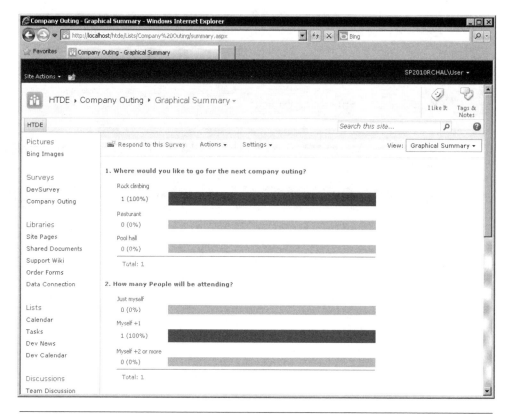

FIGURE 4-35 Viewing graphical survey results

Tip You can use the survey actions drop-down to set an alert when someone responds to your survey.

One point to note about surveys is that you can make changes as you go along. For example, you might like to send out a draft to a small audience and gather some feedback before sending out the survey link to your target audience. As you get back suggestions, you can make edits such as reordering the questions or even adding or removing questions (see Figure 4-36).

Survey Branching

You may find that you'd like to dynamically change your survey questions based on the respondents' answers. SharePoint enables this functionality with survey branching. Branching allows you to jump to a specified question based on the answer

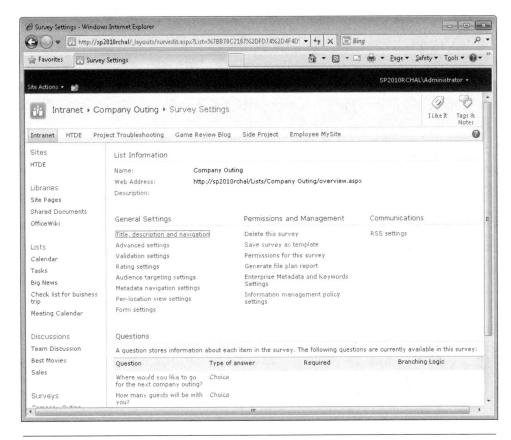

FIGURE 4-36   Survey list settings

FIGURE 4-37 Choosing branching logic for a survey question

to a different question. For example, if you're asking for opinions about dogs or cats, you can first ask which type of pet the user has at home. If the user responds that she has a cat, you can jump to a question about cats, whereas if the user says that she has a dog, you can jump to a different question, about dogs.

To enable branching, first enter your questions and then go to the survey settings, choose the question that will determine the branching, and select the target for the branch (see Figure 4-37).

Workspace Sites

The last collaboration topic is not a type of list; it's a type of site. In fact, it's more than one type of site—it's a group known as workspaces. Just like other SharePoint site templates, workspaces combine a number of features so that you don't need to go to the trouble to put them all together yourself. If web parts and lists are the ingredients, then workspaces are the house specials.

Note The application formerly known as Microsoft Groove has been renamed SharePoint Workspace. Workspace is used to work with SharePoint offline and should not be confused with the workspace site templates. The SharePoint Workspace application will be covered in more detail in Chapter 10.

Meeting Workspaces

Several different flavors of meeting workspaces come out of the box with SharePoint Server 2010, including the Basic Meeting Workspace, the Blank Meeting Workspace, the Decision Meeting Workspace, the Multipage Meeting Workspace, and the Social Meeting Workspace.

As you've already seen in this chapter and the previous chapters, there are a number of features in SharePoint that can be useful to a team that needs to meet and collaborate regularly. For example, document management allows you to work on the same documents without worrying about keeping track of which version is current, and lists such as announcement lists make it easier to publicize the latest news. Rather than having to assemble a number of standard features such as these each time you need to create a new meeting workspace, you can simply provision a new meeting workspace on your server and much of the required functionality is automatically added for you.

To create a meeting workspace, choose the More Options menu item from the Site Actions menu and then choose the Site filter. In this first example, we'll use the Basic Meeting Workspace template. When you create the site, you'll see that it is prepopulated with a list each for Objectives, Attendees, Agenda, and a Document Library (see Figure 4-38).

Other than the standard document library, the rest of these are custom lists that have been specifically chosen because they will be useful when organizing a meeting. The Objectives list makes it crystal clear what the meeting is meant to accomplish; the Attendees list shows who is invited; the Agenda list itemizes the topics; and the

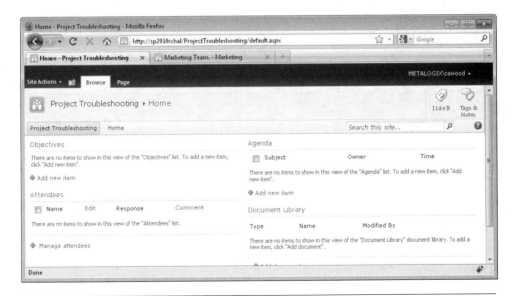

FIGURE 4-38   A meeting workspace site

Document Library allows documents related to the meeting to be shared. Some of these lists contain relatively simple information. For example, the Objectives list only requires the Description field to be completed for a new item. Others, such as the Agenda list, have multiple columns of metadata that allow for complete tracking and accountability.

Document Workspaces

Document workspace sites are designed for teams that need to collaborate on a document. As you've already seen, SharePoint offers many document management facilities such as document libraries and content approval workflow. However, just like meeting workspaces, document workspace sites put together a collection of these features and package them up into a single site template. A document workspace doesn't just consist of a Document Library; the home page of the site is a web part page that bubbles up a Tasks list, an Announcements list, and a Members web part so that you can see who is working on the project. When you create a document workspace, you'll see that the site is prepopulated with these useful lists (see Figure 4-39).

As you can see, workspaces are meant to save you the time of creating a site and then adding a bunch of lists. You may still need to do some customization to get your workspace just right for your needs, but at least the standard workspaces offer a better alternative than starting from scratch.

SharePoint Server 2010 clearly has numerous features that facilitate collaboration. This chapter covered some of that functionality. Combined with the document management features that you learned about in Chapter 3, you can take full advantage of SharePoint's collaboration functionality—it's all about teamwork.

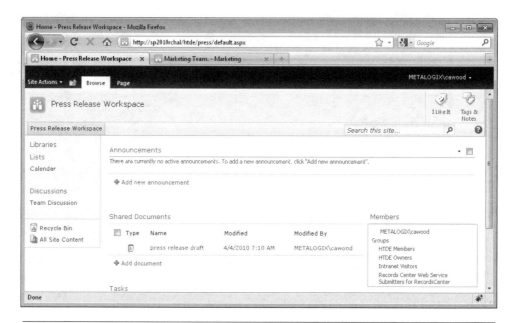

FIGURE 4-39   A new document workspace

5

Tagging and Taxonomy

HOW TO...

- Make use of social tagging
- Enable folksonomy in SharePoint
- Use managed keywords
- Use enterprise managed metadata
- Tag items with managed metadata terms
- Create a taxonomy hierarchy
- Administer a term store
- Create a new term store

Many people have questions about the new Enterprise Metadata Management (EMM), or taxonomy, features in SharePoint 2010. What's all the fuss about EMM? Why is taxonomy arguably the most important new feature in SharePoint 2010? Hasn't SharePoint always had metadata? As you'll see in this chapter, the new EMM functionality enables a number of features, including better social computing capabilities.

Facebook and Twitter have propelled social computing into mainstream acceptance, and it's not surprising that many businesses would like to be able to use social computing to accelerate collaboration and enhance knowledge management within their staff. With many social computing features already available in SharePoint and more coming with each release, a relevant question to consider is that posed by Edward Cone in the title of his 2007 article for *CIO Insight* magazine, "Will Microsoft Become Facebook for the Enterprise?" (www.cioinsight.com/c/a/ Past-News/Will-Microsoft-Become-Facebook-for-the-Enterprise/). This chapter will give you a sense of why the question was asked—as you'll see, SharePoint is well on the way.

 Note SharePoint My Sites, which were available in SharePoint Portal Server 2003, were available before Facebook was launched in 2004.

There are two types of taxonomy available in SharePoint Server 2010:

- **Managed**   This is a centrally managed and controlled tagging system. The benefit is that the tags can be guaranteed to fit into a rigid taxonomy. However, this type of system needs to be properly planned and built before users can start applying tags.
- **Social tagging (a.k.a. folksonomy)**   This is a loose system that can lead to varied results. On the positive side, people are free to use a taxonomy that makes sense to them, and because people define their own terms, they may find items easier. However, issues are likely to arise where slightly different terms are used to tag items that really should all have the same tags.

This chapter discusses both types of taxonomy and how they are used in SharePoint Server 2010.

Social Tagging

One aspect of social computing that SharePoint lacked in the past is social tagging. SharePoint Server 2010 comes with a few improvements in this area. The first of these that you might notice in SharePoint 2010 are the "I Like It" and "Tags & Notes" options that appear in the top-right of many SharePoint web pages.

These options allow you to bubble up content that is interesting in some way as well as classify it for easier retrieval down the line. Recall that in Chapter 4 you saw how you can create discussion boards to carry on conversations with other SharePoint users. Now suppose that you've come across an interesting thread and you'd like to not only share it with your co-workers, but also make it easier for you to find in the future.

I Like It

The first option for SharePoint social tagging is the simple-to-use I Like It tag. All you have to do is go to any SharePoint item that you'd like to tag, select it from the list, and then click the I Like It button in the ribbon—it's that simple (see Figure 5-1).

Ratings

There may be times when you would like to gather feedback about which documents are the most useful or the best suited for a particular purpose. SharePoint ratings can help you gather this data.

If you would like to allow users to assign a value to items in a list, you can enable the ratings option. To turn ratings on for a list, go to the list settings, and under General Settings click on Rating settings. Once you have navigated to the Rating Settings page, you can simply click the radio buttons to enable or disable the rating option.

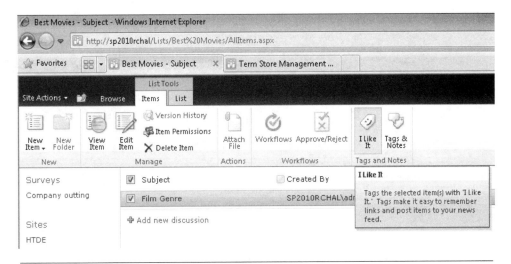

FIGURE 5-1   Using the I Like It tag

My Profile

When you have tagged something with I Like It, the action will appear in the news feed for your profile (if this option is enabled). In this way, you can share your choices and your social network will benefit from your tagging activities.

You can also add information to your profile page to both make your SharePoint experience more personal and help other people in your organization figure out your expertise and interests. Microsoft uses this information to allow employees to track down subject matter experts when they have questions. For example, someone with a SharePoint question can use the information to find a SharePoint expert. The profile also includes an organization browser so that you can see who works on specific teams.

 The organization browser is just one of the many features in SharePoint 2010 that take advantage of Microsoft's Silverlight technology. If you install Silverlight, your experience in SharePoint is more visually appealing.

Other actions—such as adding notes—can also appear in your news feed. To view what you've tagged and see your news feed, go to the top right of a SharePoint web page and expand the drop-down menu under your username. From there, choose My Profile to view or edit your profile page (see Figure 5-2).

Once you have your profile page open, you can click the links on the Tags and Notes tab to view the items that you've tagged (see Figure 5-3).

You'll notice that there are actually two links for notes, Public and Private, so that you can choose whether or not you want your notes to be publicly visible. This is a nice segue to the next topic: Tags & Notes.

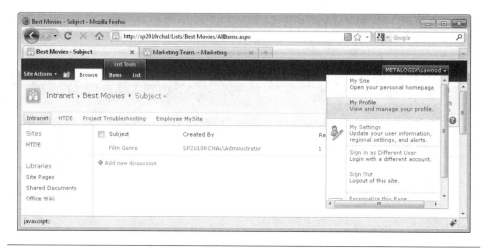

FIGURE 5-2 Opening a profile page

FIGURE 5-3 Viewing my tags in my profile

Tags & Notes

Similar to choosing the I Like It tag, you can also make up your own tags and apply those to SharePoint items. These types of tags aren't predetermined, so you can make up tags for whatever you need. This open taxonomy is referred to as a *folksonomy*, and you'll learn more about it in the "Managed Keywords" section of this chapter. For now, you can think of Tags & Notes as another open taxonomy option.

To apply your own custom tags to an item, select the item and then click Tags & Notes on the ribbon to open the dialog shown in Figure 5-4. You can then start typing keywords to tag the item. After you have tagged some things, go back to your profile page and check what appears in your news feed and under the Tags and Notes section.

Just like tags, you can add notes by selecting your target item and choosing Tags & Notes. When the dialog opens, click the Note Board tab to enter your notes (see Figure 5-5). Notes allow you to store more information about an item. Instead of a word or phrase, you'll be able to write 250 characters and store that information with the item. You may want to do this to keep track of your thoughts, or you may want to keep track of related information by pasting in a link. What you do with notes is up to you.

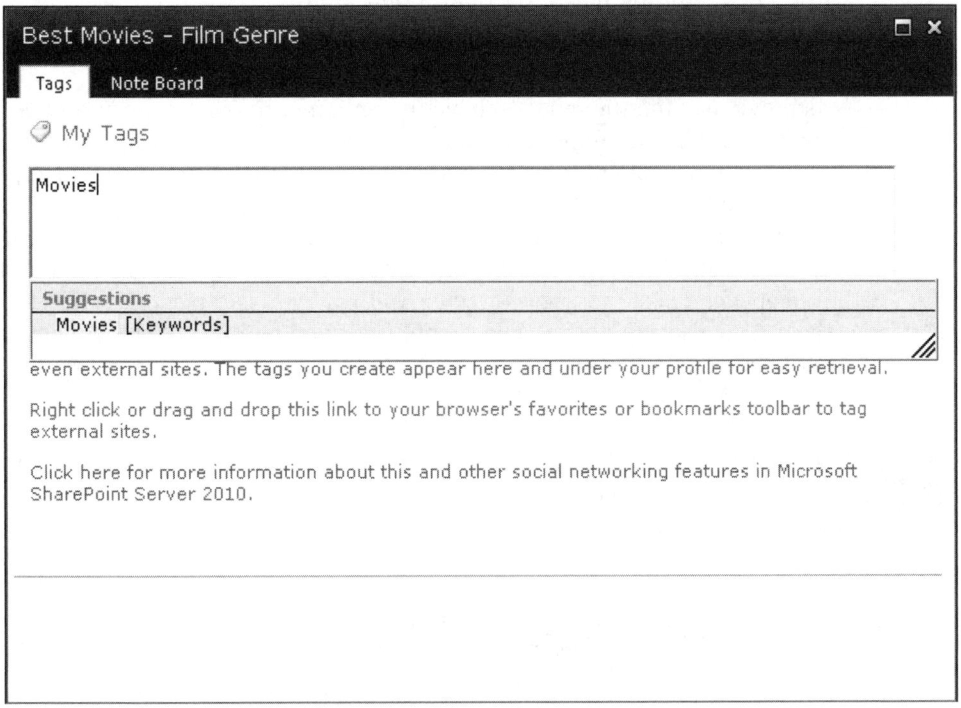

FIGURE 5-4   Tagging an item with a personal tag

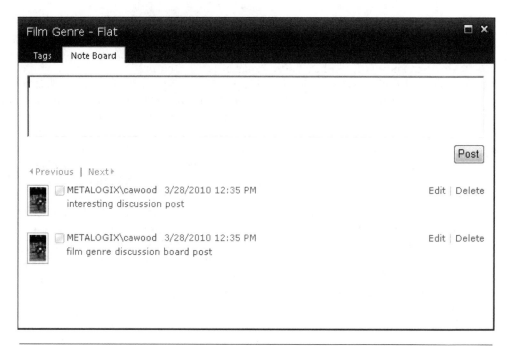

FIGURE 5-5 Adding notes to a SharePoint item

As previously mentioned, you have the option of making your notes public or private. If you make them private, you will be able to view them in your profile, but no one else will be able to read them. If you make them public, they will appear in your news feed and everyone will be able to benefit from your insights.

In addition to tagging items with notes, you will also have a note board on your profile page. This note board is similar to a user's wall in a Facebook account. Other people can post messages on your wall, and you can respond with your own messages. You also can post updates about what you're doing so that others can read your note board and follow your progress. Either way, you have the ability to interact with other SharePoint users via your note board.

 My Sites and Profiles are SharePoint Server 2010 features—they are not available in SharePoint Foundation 2010.

Enterprise Managed Metadata

The Microsoft TechNet Library article "Managed Metadata Overview (SharePoint Server 2010)" defines managed metadata as follows: "*Managed metadata* is a hierarchical collection of centrally managed terms that you can define, and then use as attributes for items in Microsoft SharePoint Server 2010." (See http://technet .microsoft.com/en-us/library/ee424402(office.14).aspx.) Managed terms and keywords can be used to enhance or enable a number of features within SharePoint. For example, using the taxonomy created by managed terms, users can have a more powerful search experience.

SharePoint 2010 Taxonomy Improvements

While it's true that SharePoint has always provided the option to associate metadata with the data stored in SharePoint, before EMM, organizations using SharePoint would have to either build their own taxonomy solution or rely upon business rules for how their users should add metadata. This meant that different users could tag items with slightly different terms, thereby eliminating most of the value of taxonomy. There were also technical constraints that prevented creation of a custom solution. For example, the logical place to store terms would be in a list, but lists couldn't be shared across site collection boundaries, so the taxonomy would have to be duplicated if you wanted to share terms. There was also no concept of hierarchical metadata and no way to share a collection of terms with delegated permissions. All of these issues have been resolved in SharePoint Server 2010, but if you want to understand the importance of the changes made in SharePoint 2010, SharePoint MVP Chris O'Brien wrote a whole post called "Managed Metadata in SharePoint 2010—some notes on the "why," about why SharePoint 2010 taxonomy is important (www.sharepointnutsandbolts.com), and the TechNet Library article just quoted includes the section "Benefits of Using Managed Metadata," which lists and describes the following benefits:

More consistent use of terminology

Managed metadata facilitates more consistent use of terms, as well as more consistent use of the managed keywords that are added to SharePoint Server items. You can pre-define terms, and allow only authorized users to add new terms. You can also prohibit users from adding their own managed keywords to items and require them to use existing ones. Managed metadata also provides greater accuracy by presenting only a list of correct terms from which users can select values. Because managed keywords are also a type of managed metadata, even the managed keywords that users apply to items can be more consistent.

Because metadata is used more consistently, you can have a higher degree of confidence that it is correct. When you use metadata to automate business processes—for example, placing documents in different files in the record center based on the value of their department attribute—you can be confident that the metadata was created by authorized users, and that the value of the department attribute is always one of the valid values.

Better search results

A simple search can provide more relevant results if items have consistent attributes.

As users apply managed terms and keywords to items, they are guided to terms that have already been used. In some cases, users might not even be able to enter a new value. Because users are focused on a specific set of terms, those terms—and not synonyms—are more likely to be applied to items. Searching for a managed term or a managed keyword is, therefore, likely to retrieve more relevant results.

Dynamic

In previous versions of SharePoint Server, to restrict the value of an attribute to being one of a set of values, you would have created a column whose type is "choice," and then provided a list of valid values. When you needed to add a new value to set of choices, you would have to modify every column that used the same set of values.

By using managed metadata in SharePoint Server 2010, you can separate the set of valid values from the columns whose value must be one of the set of valid values. When you need to add a new value, you add a term to the term set, and all columns that map to that term set would use the updated set of choices.

Using terms can help you keep SharePoint Server items in sync with the business as the business changes. For example, assume your company's new product had a code name early in its development and was given an official name shortly before the product launched. You included a term for the code name in the "product" term set, and users have been identifying all documents related to the product by using the term. When the product name changed, you could edit the term and change its name to the product's official name. The term is still applied to the same items, but its name is now updated.

To borrow a joke from Dan Kogan, Microsoft SharePoint Program Manager, delivered during his SharePoint Conference 2009 talk, "when we talk about terms, we need to first define our terms." The following definitions are adapted from the MSDN Library article "Managing Metadata" (http://msdn.microsoft.com/en-us/library/ee559337(office.14).aspx):

- **Term**   A word or phrase that can be associated with an item in SharePoint Server 2010.
- **Term set**   A collection of related terms.
- **Managed terms**   Terms that can be created only by users with the appropriate permissions, and are often organized into a hierarchy. Managed terms are usually predefined.
- **Managed keywords**   Words or phrases that have been added to SharePoint Server 2010 items. All managed keywords (also called enterprise keywords) are part of a single, non-hierarchical term set called the keyword set.
- **Term store**   A database that stores both managed terms and managed keywords. The Term Store Management Tool is available in Central Administration (and Site Settings). This tool manages terms centrally for the whole farm and can be used to create, copy, reuse, move, duplicate (for polyhierarchy), deprecate, delete, and

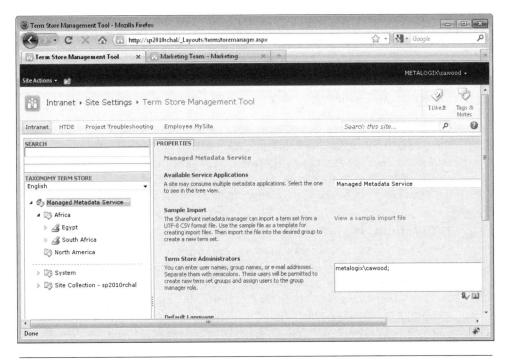

FIGURE 5-6   The Term Store Management Tool

merge terms (see Figure 5-6). The Term Store Management Tool is also used to manage permissions on term stores.

A polyhierarchy-enabled tree can include leaves (nodes) that have more than one branch (parent node). In SharePoint Server 2010, you can create a polyhierarchical structure with the Reuse Terms action in the Term Store Management Tool. For example, imagine that you have a taxonomy of people terms, and the term sets define teams to which they belong. A person could be on more than one team and, therefore, you might want to reuse terms rather than copy them (and potentially have them become out of synch if edits occur down the line).

Also, one important definition that isn't in the article:

- **Group**   In the term store, all term sets are created within groups. In other words, *group* is the parent container for term sets.

A Taxonomy Primer

Before you set out to use the SharePoint EMM functionality, it's important to have an understanding of taxonomy at a higher level. In case you aren't a library scientist or a taxonomist, this section offers a quick introduction to some taxonomy concepts. Taxonomy relationships are commonly divided into three types:

- Equivalent (synonyms: "LOL" is equivalent to "laughing out loud")
- Hierarchical (parent/child: "sports equipment" is the parent node of "ball")
- Associative (concept/concept: "bouncy things" is related to "ball")

SharePoint 2010 provides SharePoint users, administrators, and developers with the UI and application programming interface (API) required for the first two types of relationships. This means that faculties such as centrally managed terms, folksonomy, and Tag Clouds (social tagging) are enabled. The third type—which SharePoint 2010 does not offer—is associative relationships. Here's a quick discussion of each type.

Equivalent Terms

SharePoint taxonomy allows synonyms and preferred terms. Synonyms allow a central understanding that LOL is the same as "laughing out loud," and preferred terms specify which of the two should be used.

The other side of the equivalence coin is dealing with words with more than one meaning. To help disambiguate terms, SharePoint term descriptions are displayed in a tooltip so that users can differentiate between *G-Force* (the recent movie featuring a specially trained squad of guinea pigs) and G-Force from *Battle of the Planets* (a cartoon from the 1980s).

Another aspect of equivalency is multilingual considerations. If you are tagging in different languages, there's a good chance that you'll want to create a relationship between words that actually mean the same thing.

Hierarchical Terms

A central repository of terms enables consistency across users. Providing a hierarchy allows for information architecture and organization. In the SharePoint Term Store Management Tool, users with sufficient permissions will be able to perform many operations on terms in the hierarchy. The hierarchy is broken down into a term store at the top, then a group, then term sets, and, finally, managed terms.

Associative Terms

Associative terms are used to create ontologies. There are endless possibilities for these types of relationships. For example, you could have a hierarchy of terms in SharePoint 2010 that includes the terms "ball" and "bat" as children of the term "sports equipment." An ontology would allow you to also create a relationship between "bouncy things" and "ball" because they are conceptually related.

Why didn't the SharePoint team add ontologies? That's a reasonable question, but the fact is that tackling such a specialized function simply might not have been worth the effort when the team was already trying to build an ambitious feature. Also, I've heard people wonder aloud whether anyone but a library scientist or a taxonomist will complain.

Managed Keywords

There are two types of tags in the new SharePoint 2010 EMM system: managed keywords and managed terms. You have already seen managed keywords in action in the "Social Tagging" section earlier in this chapter; now you'll see how those tags fit in with the overall taxonomy strategy in SharePoint 2010. In this section, you'll see examples of how users can take advantage of the various features that each type of tagging enables. Managed terms are covered in the next section.

Managed keywords (or just "keywords") are used for user-focused tagging. Users decide which keywords they want to add to the system and what needs to be tagged. This type of open tagging is called a "folksonomy" because it's created by people instead of laid out by the organization. In this way, keywords are used to informally tag content within SharePoint.

 Unlike managed terms, managed keywords do not have a hierarchical structure.

You've already seen one way to add keywords to a SharePoint item—using the Tags & Notes dialog. Another way to add keywords is to edit the properties on an item. In this example, you'll add a managed keyword to a document in a document library.

Enabling Keywords

If keywords have not been enabled on the document library, you need to click on the Library tab in the ribbon and then click Library Settings. Once you are at the Document Library Settings page, look for the Enterprise Metadata and Keywords Settings link under the Permissions and Management settings category. Click the link and you'll be offered the choice to enable enterprise keywords (see Figure 5-7).

In this dialog, you also are given the option to add the keywords and terms that are associated with the items in this library to My Site profiles. If you select this option, that data will appear in Tag Cloud web parts and on profile pages. To add a managed term to a document, first select the document in the document library and select Edit Properties from the drop-down menu (see Figure 5-8).

Once you have the edit document properties dialog open, find the Enterprise Keywords field and start typing either an existing keyword (in which case you will be prompted with suggestions as you type) or a new keyword (see Figure 5-9).

 Managed keywords (or just keywords) are primarily used for social tagging, such as in Tag Clouds and folksonomy, but keywords can be promoted to managed terms using the Term Store Management Tool. This topic is covered later in this chapter.

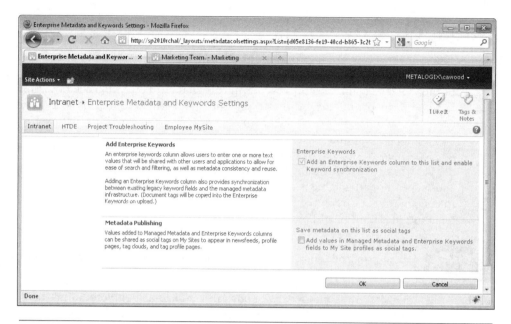

FIGURE 5-7 Enabling keywords on a document library

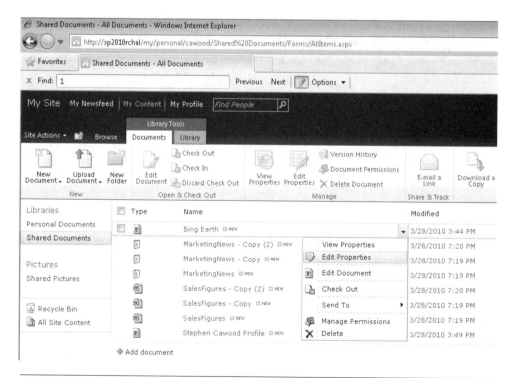

FIGURE 5-8 Selecting a document to edit its properties

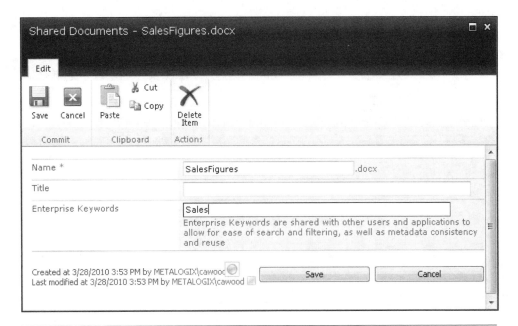

FIGURE 5-9   Adding a keyword to a document

Using the Tag Cloud Web Part

Once you've begun tagging things, you'll probably want to be able to use that data in convenient ways. The Tag Cloud web part is a quick way to view the folksonomy being created on your SharePoint server.

If you have sufficient permissions to create a web part page and add web parts, you'll be able to add the Tag Cloud web part to web part pages. To add the web part, click the Edit Page button on the ribbon and then click an Add a Web Part link within the page. Once you do this, the add web part page will open (see Figure 5-10). Select Tag Cloud from the list of web parts and click Add.

After you add the web part, you will immediately see it appear on the page (see Figure 5-11).

The relative sizes of the terms indicate how popular they are on the server. In this example, the Movies term has been added more than the others (see Figure 5-12).

If you choose to edit the web part, you will find a number of options in the Tag Cloud settings. For example, you can choose to only show your tags, or to show tags from all users.

Many features can be deactivated at the site collection level. If you find that you're not offered the Tag Cloud web part or some other out-of-the-box web part, ask your SharePoint administrator to investigate. Also, as you learned earlier, these features aren't available in SharePoint Foundation 2010.

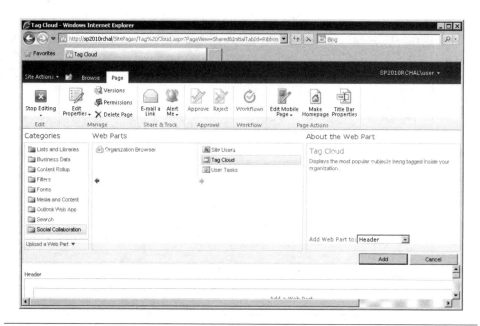

FIGURE 5-10 Choosing to add the Tag Cloud web part to a page

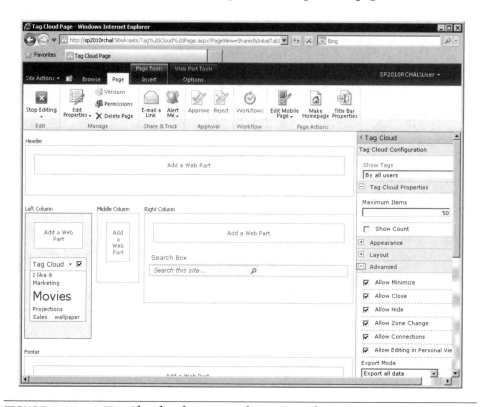

FIGURE 5-11 A Tag Cloud web part in edit page mode

FIGURE 5-12   The Tag Cloud web part in action

Managed Terms

Managed terms are the other type of tags in SharePoint 2010 EMM. Unlike managed keywords, managed terms are placed in a controlled central repository. This enables consistency across users, provides hierarchical organization, and allows for strict information architecture. In the SharePoint Term Store Management Tool, users with sufficient permissions are able to perform many operations on terms in the hierarchy. However, most users will simply use the terms from the central store.

As with keywords, terms can be added to many types of content within SharePoint. The following example will show you how to add a term to a document within a document library that has already been enabled for tagging with terms.

To add a managed term to a document, first select the document in the document library and select Edit Properties from the drop-down menu. Once you have the edit document properties dialog open, find the Managed Metadata field and either start typing a term or click the Browse for a valid choice icon on the right. This will open the Select Managed Metadata dialog (see Figure 5-13).

 Terms can be labeled with a description that helps users figure out which term to use.

Metadata-Driven Navigation

Managed metadata can be used to enable some cool navigational features within SharePoint 2010. For example, if you go to a list that has a managed metadata column, you'll be able to filter the view by simply selecting one of the terms being used in the list (see Figure 5-14). This enables the end user to instantly filter lists without

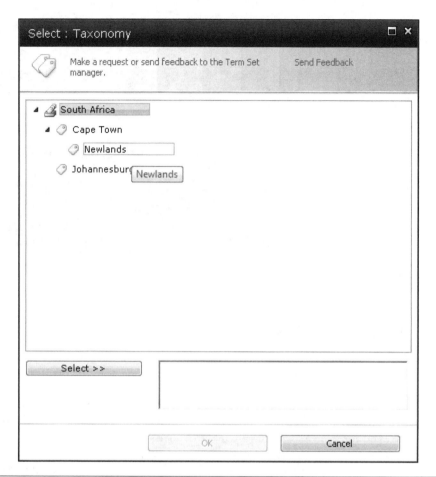

FIGURE 5-13 Browsing for a term to add to a document

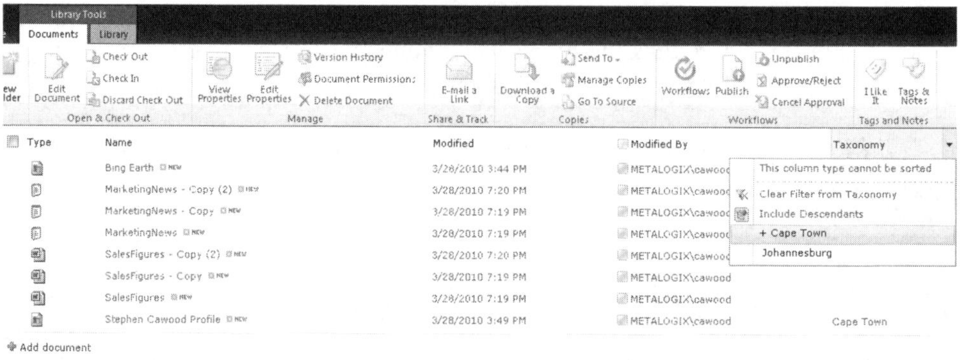

FIGURE 5-14 Filtering a document library using the managed metadata term "Cape Town"

having to create a custom view. Later in this chapter, you'll learn how to enable this functionality on your lists.

Once you apply the filter, the column heading will show a funnel icon to indicate that you're not seeing the full list.

SharePoint Managed Metadata Administration

If you need to administer SharePoint taxonomy, the first step will be to learn how to use SharePoint term stores and research the details for creating a SharePoint taxonomy hierarchy. You'll also want to read Microsoft's best practices and make use of the managed metadata planning data sheets. To ensure that you end up with the best possible taxonomy for your organization, you'll likely want to collaborate with some business users so that you can determine the best possible terms, terms sets, and groups.

After you have set up your term store and decided how your taxonomy will be organized, you'll need to set the permissions on your term store and enable various content for tagging. Remember that there are two types of tagging: managed keywords and managed metadata. Managed keywords are used for informal "folksonomy" style tagging, and managed terms are used for centrally controlled and delegated hierarchical term structures.

Enabling Managed Metadata on Your Server

In the new SharePoint 2010 EMM features, all taxonomy data is stored within a SQL Server database called the term store. Creating a managed service application creates a term store that you can use to build your taxonomy hierarchy.

Here are the steps to enable managed term tagging on a SharePoint list or library:

1. Add an administrator to your term store.
2. Create some terms.
3. Add a column of type "Managed Metadata" to the list or library.

When you first go to the Term Store Management Tool , you'll find that you don't have any options to create or manage terms. The reason for this is that you need to add yourself to the administrators group for the managed metadata service. To open the Term Store Management tool, you can either go to Central Administration | Application Management | Manage Service Applications | Managed Metadata Service or Site Settings | Site Administration | Term Store Management. There options will both open the same Term Store Management Tool interface (see Figure 5-15).

When the term store page is open, you can use the SharePoint People Picker to add administrators in the Term Store Administrators section (see Figure 5-16).

After you add yourself and save the changes, you'll be able to create groups, term sets, and terms (see Figure 5-17).

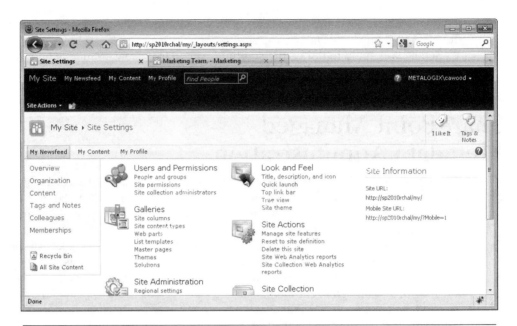

FIGURE 5-15 Opening the Term Store Management Tool in Site Settings

At this point, you can try to tag SharePoint content. If you open a list and try to tag something, and you see the message, "This control is currently disabled. You might not have the right permission level to use this, you might need to select an object or item, or the content might not work in this context," then you either have a rights issue or have another problem with your server (see Figure 5-18).

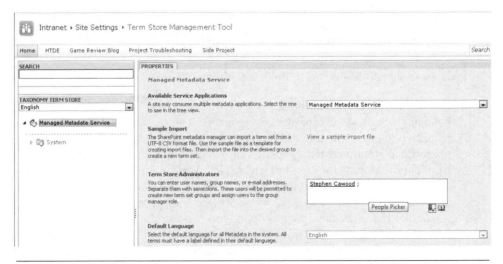

FIGURE 5-16 Adding an administrator to the term store

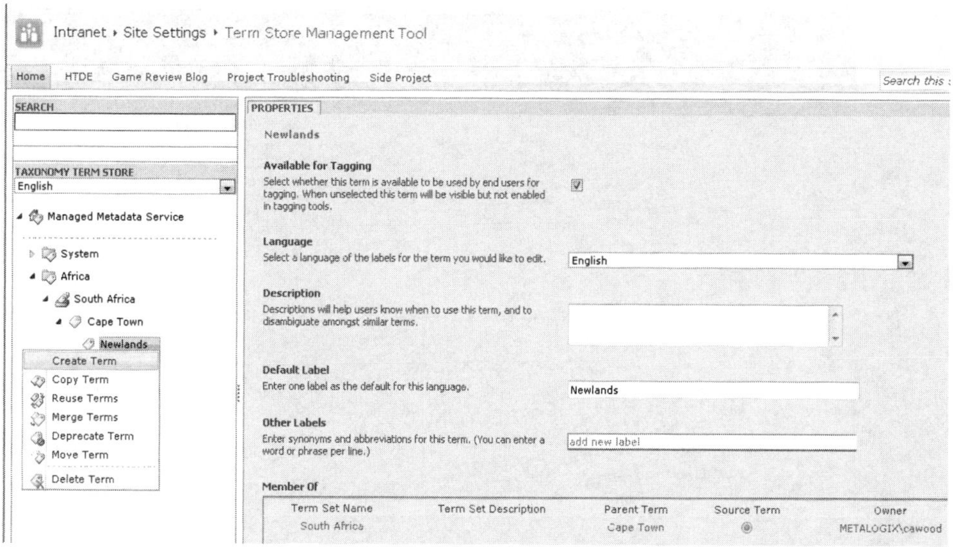

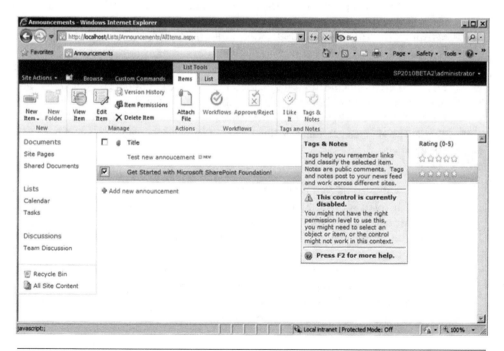

FIGURE 5-17   Once you add yourself as an administrator, you can start to use the term store.

FIGURE 5-18   Tagging control disabled in the ribbon

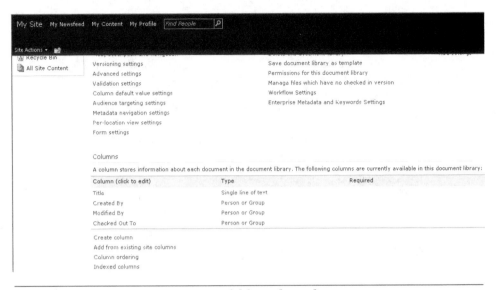

FIGURE 5-19 Create Column is available in the Columns section

To use managed terms, you'll need to add a new column to your lists and libraries. This column will store the managed term data. To add the column, go to the list you want to enable, choose the Library tab from the ribbon, and then choose Library Settings from the Settings area. On the Library Settings page, scroll down to the Columns section and choose Create Column (see Figure 5-19).

When the Create Column dialog opens, choose the Managed Metadata column type and give the column a name (see Figure 5-20). You'll also be able to choose options such as whether you want to allow multiple values.

The Managed Metadata column can allow multiple values if you choose to allow them.

You will also have the option of filtering the available taxonomy tree down to a particular term set (see Figure 5-21).

After adding this column, you can edit the properties of a document in the document library and see a new option to choose managed terms to put into the new managed metadata field. You have two options for adding terms. The first is to start typing in the field, which prompts SharePoint to suggest tags that match the characters you have typed (see Figure 5-22). The other option is to click the little tags icon on the right of the field, which enables you to browse your term store.

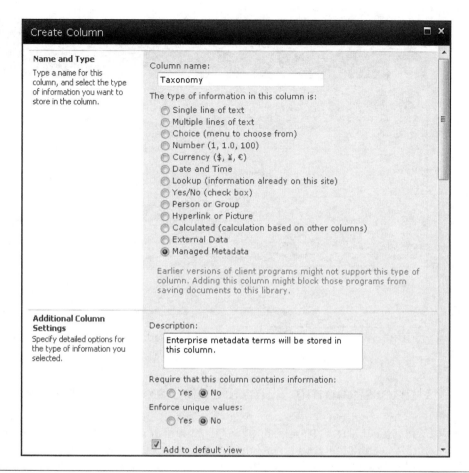

FIGURE 5-20   Use the Managed Metadata column type for managed terms

FIGURE 5-21   Filtering the column to a term set

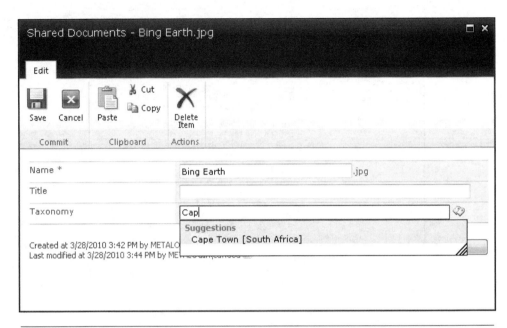

FIGURE 5-22 After adding the managed metadata column, terms can be added.

Understanding SharePoint Taxonomy Hierarchy

If you're wondering how to organize your SharePoint 2010 EMM, you should start by reading the TechNet article, "Plan Terms and Term Sets (SharePoint Server 2010)" (http://technet.microsoft.com/en-us/library/ee519604(office.14).aspx). This section highlights some of the key points of that article and also adds a few points from other sources.

While the TechNet article reminds you that you could simply allow your users to add keywords and then use their input to create your taxonomy—promoting keywords to managed terms as necessary—it seems likely that most organizations will want to start with an organized metadata hierarchy.

 Unlike managed terms, managed keywords are stored in a nonhierarchical fashion.

As you've already learned, SharePoint 2010 EMM managed terms are organized into a hierarchy. The objects within this hierarchy are term stores, groups, term sets, and terms. These are the rules for the taxonomy hierarchy:

- When a managed metadata service is created, a term store will be created. Once you have a term store, you can create a group. A group is a security boundary.
- Once you have a group, you can create a term set. A term set must be the child of a single parent group.

- Under a term set, terms can be created. A term can be the child of a term set, or of another term.
- A term can be added as a child of another term.
- Terms can be nested to seven levels.

The previously referenced TechNet article "Plan Terms and Term Sets (SharePoint Server 2010)" clearly states that "You can nest terms to a maximum of seven levels deep." However, at the time of writing, the latest SharePoint Server 2010 build does not enforce this constraint.

One of the key points of the TechNet article about planning your terms and term sets is that a group is a security boundary. A group contributor can manage the term sets in the groups and create new term sets. All users who have access to a term set under a group can see all of the other term sets—even if they don't have rights to manage the other term sets. Based on this, you should organize your term sets into groups based on the groups of users who will manage them. For this reason, your taxonomy may correlate to your organizational structure. Take a look at the example shown in Figure 5-23, which has the following hierarchy:

- **Term store**   The term store is simply titled "Taxonomy."

You can have multiple terms stores. Each term store is stored in a separate SQL Server database.

- **Groups**   Under the term store are two groups: Africa and North America. The idea is that these could be significant geographical locations to this particular fictional organization. Remember that the groups are a security boundary, so the users assigned to the Africa group don't have to have any access to the North America group. However, if users are given rights to a term set under one of the groups, they will be able to see the names of all the term sets under that group.
- **Term sets**   Inside the Africa group there are two term sets: South Africa and Egypt.
- **Terms**   At the top level, the South Africa term set contains the terms Cape Town and Johannesburg. In this case, the Cape Town term contains the child term Newlands (a neighborhood in Cape Town), and that term contains the child term Ravensberg Avenue.

When you're creating your managed terms, you're free to identify synonyms; you can also specify which is the preferred term, so that when a user types in "Joburg," for example, she will be asked to assign the term "Johannesburg."

You can specify a custom sort order for terms, so it isn't necessary to show them in alphabetical order.

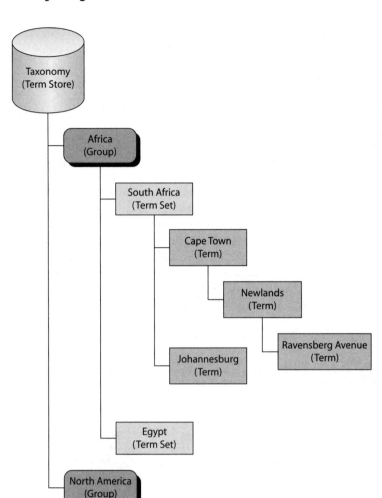

FIGURE 5-23 Example SharePoint 2010 EMM hierarchy

Term sets can be open or closed. Open sets allow all users to add terms. Terms can be added to closed sets only by users who are contributors to the group. As you've seen, in addition to terms, SharePoint 2010 EMM contains keywords. Keywords aren't restricted, and that's why they can be used informally to create folksonomy.

If you've been tasked with creating the taxonomy for your EMM hierarchy, the points outlined in this section are important, but I strongly recommend that you also take advantage of the articles and the planning worksheets available on TechNet. Setting up a taxonomy is a potentially complex task, and a lack of proper planning or a poorly designed taxonomy could be worse than not having one at all.

Promoting a Managed Keyword to a Managed Term

One philosophy for building out a taxonomy hierarchy is to let the users decide which terms are important. In SharePoint 2010, there are two ways to achieve this. First, you can allow "fill in" keywords in your term sets. Secondly, you can allow users to tag with managed keywords and then you can choose to promote some (or all) of them to managed terms.

To change a managed keyword to a managed term, you simply open the Term Store Management Tool (from Central Administration or Site Settings) and use the Move option to move the keyword into the term hierarchy. To access the Move action, right-click on the term that you'd like to move (see Figure 5-24).

 It is not possible to move a managed term to the keywords store. In other words, you can promote a managed keyword to a managed term, but you can't demote a managed term to a keyword.

Creating Your Own Term Store

If you want to create your own term store, you'll need to follow the steps provided in this section to create a new managed metadata service. Generally, this won't be necessary because one term store will be enough for most organizations.

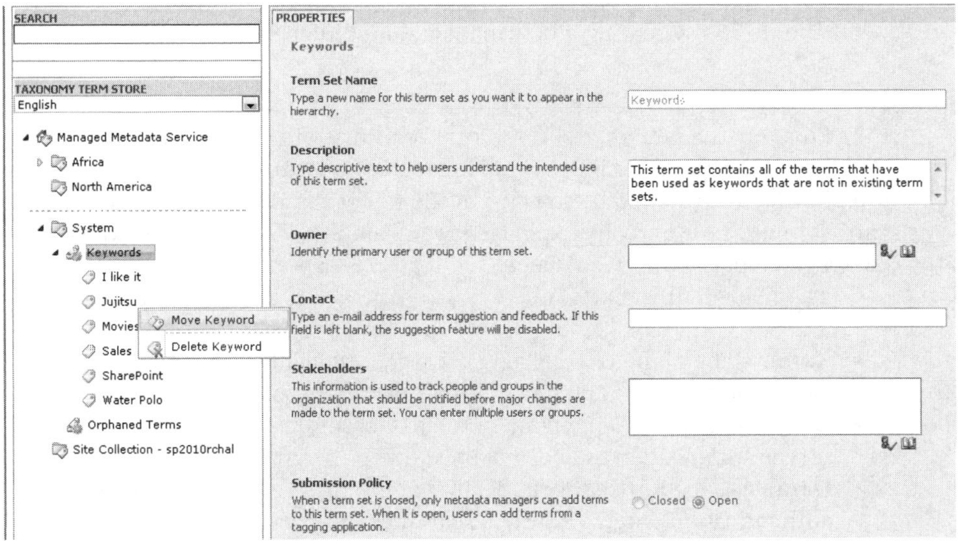

FIGURE 5-24   Moving a keyword to the term store will convert it to a managed term.

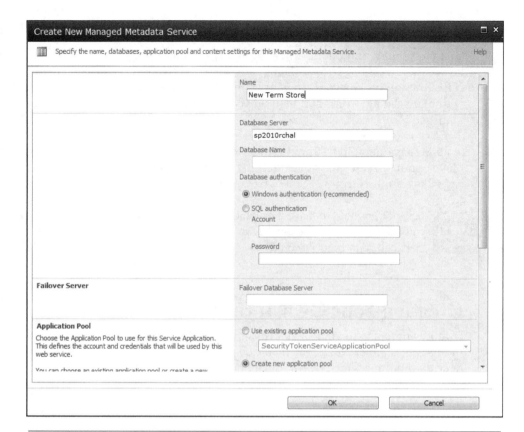

FIGURE 5-25 Creating a new managed metadata service

First, open SharePoint 2010 Central Administration and select Manage Service Applications from the Application Management section. At this point, the Service Applications tab should be selected at the top of the page. Next, click the drop-down arrow under New and click Managed Metadata Service. This opens the Create New Managed Metadata Service dialog (see Figure 5-25).

The fields in this dialog are

- **Name**   The name of your new managed metadata service.
- **Database Server**   The name of your database server.
- **Database Name**   The name of the database you want to use on the selected server. If the database does not exist, it will be created.
- **Database authentication**   The recommended option is Windows authentication, but SQL authentication is also available.

- **Failover Database Server** If you're using a failover database server, you can enter it here.
- **Application Pool** You can either create a new pool or choose an existing one from the drop-down menu. Note: Ensure that the selected application pool is actually running before you try to use your term store.
- **Content Type Hub** From Microsoft: "If you want the managed metadata service to provide access to a content type library as well as to a term store, type the URL of the site collection that contains the content type library in the Content Type hub box. The service will share the content type library at the root of the site collection."

From the same area of Central Administration, you have options to perform numerous other operations on your term store. For example, you can delete a term store, modify the term store permissions, add term store administrators, and more (see Figure 5-26).

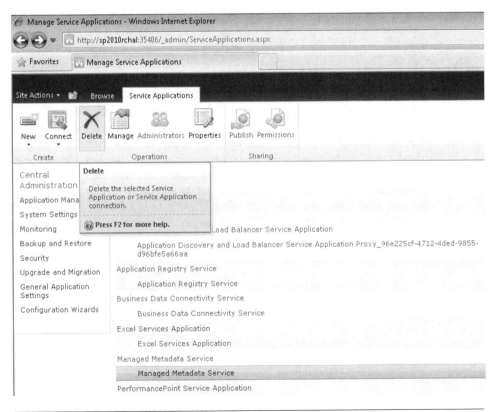

FIGURE 5-26 The ribbon offers more term store management options.

How Will the New SharePoint 2010 Taxonomy Be Used?

Obviously, the most popular end-user application of EMM will be building a taxonomy to fulfill business needs and social tagging. If keyword tagging and managed term tagging is enabled, users will be able to tag their list items, documents, and so forth with open keywords or centrally managed terms. This end-user associated metadata will then be used to classify, organize, find, and share information within SharePoint. By tagging external pages, users have a way to add links to their favorite browser's bookmarks.

However, another aspect of the new managed metadata functionality is how it can be used for enhanced navigation and search. For example, terms can be used to enable more advanced parametric search features, filtering, and targeted search. One thing is for sure, customers and partners will find interesting ways to use the taxonomy framework.

In terms of navigation, the ability to alter the way you navigate your data based on tags is also referred to as faceted navigation. When I was working on Microsoft Office SharePoint Server 2007 navigation, we nicknamed faceted navigation, "navigation goggles," the idea being that you could choose different types of navigation the same way you can shift between song view, albums, or artists on many MP3 players.

The Term Store Management Tool available in Central Administration (and Site Settings) enables administrators to manage a central vocabulary of terms for the whole farm. Operations that administrators can perform on the term hierarchy include copying, reusing, moving, duplicating, deprecating, and merging. Furthermore, having a managed repository enforces consistency across users.

The new SharePoint 2010 EMM functionality is exciting and provides options for centrally managed taxonomies as well as social tagging. Through managed metadata, SharePoint users gain access to functionality such as folksonomy, Tag Clouds, list filtering, and more powerful search options.

6

Publishing Sites

HOW TO...

- Use publishing sites to create web pages
- Work with page layouts
- Change the site master page
- Create a publishing site with workflow
- Create and format a publishing page

It's no secret that SharePoint was originally targeted at internal websites (that is, intranets). However, over the last couple of releases, Microsoft has been working to break SharePoint out of the internal server box. SharePoint publishing sites allow you to create and edit pages that are more akin to the web pages that most people associate with their favorite Internet sites. Lately, more and more companies have chosen to use the SharePoint for Internet Sites license option to create public-facing websites in SharePoint. For example, the impressive-looking Ferrari website runs on SharePoint (www.ferrari.com).

As well as allowing you to create web pages, publishing sites offer many useful features that are enabled by the SharePoint framework. For example, you'll be able to use content approval workflow or require users to check out pages before they can be edited. All of these features help to maintain a consistent publishing process.

Publishing Site Template

The publishing templates are a big part of web content management (WCM) with SharePoint. WCM is such a huge topic that an entire book could be written about SharePoint WCM; in fact, Microsoft MVP Andrew Connell did just that with his book *Professional SharePoint 2007 Web Content Management Development* (Wrox, 2008). In this section, we'll take a look at the publishing site templates and some of the options they enable.

Naturally, the first step for this exercise is to create a publishing site. If you've read the previous chapters, you know that you have a few options for creating a new site

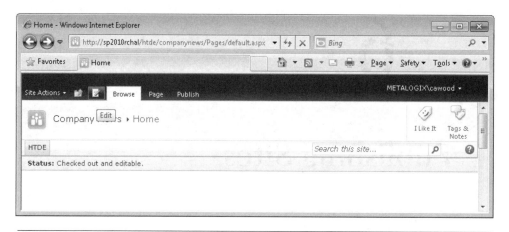

FIGURE 6-1 A new publishing site

under the current site: you can choose Site Actions | Create Site; you can choose Site Actions | More Options; or you can click All Site Content from the bottom of the quick launch and then click the Create link. Either way, you'll need to have sufficient rights to create a new site. Once you have selected the Publishing Site template and given your new site a name and a URL address, you can click the Create button and SharePoint will provision a site that you can use to try the examples in this section (see Figure 6-1). The reason you are given a chance to enter both a name and a URL is that you may want to use an abbreviation for the URL. For example, spaces will be converted to "%20" in a URL, so many users choose to eliminate the spaces that appear in the name.

 The Quick Launch setting option will change to "Navigation" once you have publishing enabled. You won't find Quick Launch in the Site Settings options after publishing is enabled.

Before you can make changes to your publishing pages, you need to switch to edit mode, and that leads right into the next topic.

Editing a Page

To enter edit mode from the publishing site home page, you can simply click the little edit icon in the top left of the page—it looks like a page with a pencil lying across it. You can also click the Page tab on the ribbon and then click Edit Page. When you switch to edit mode, you will see that a wealth of functionality is available for your publishing pages (see Figure 6-2).

The most obvious edits that you might want to make would be in the Page Content section of the page (where the cursor is located in Figure 6-2). You'll be able to use various editing features such as spell check and markup styles.

You also have quick access to the Title and Page Image areas. For example, you can simply click the link to set the page image and then browse your SharePoint server for the link to use as the page image (see Figure 6-3).

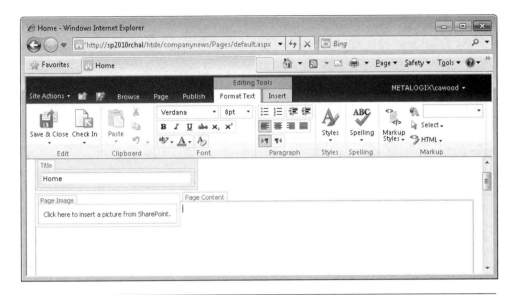

FIGURE 6-2   A publishing page in edit mode

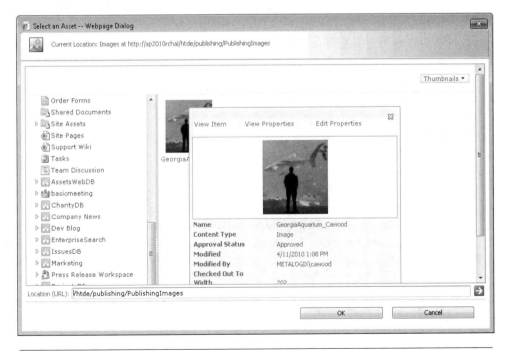

FIGURE 6-3   Browsing to select a page image

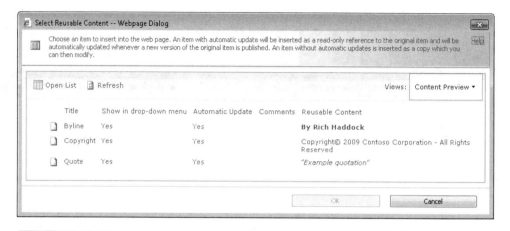

FIGURE 6-4 The Reusable Content list

When you have the page in edit mode, you'll also be able to use the Insert tab options. These include options to add tables, pictures, audio, video, links, files, and web parts. You can also add items from the Reusable Content list. For example, you might want to have a standard copyright notice or signature that can be easily reused. If you choose the More Choices option from the Reusable Content menu, you'll be shown the current content in the list, and also be able to open the list to add more (see Figure 6-4).

After you've edited your page, don't forget to click the Save & Close button. If the page requires check-in, you'll also need to check it in before it can be published. Your changes won't be visible to users who only have read access until you have published the page. Use the Publish tab in the ribbon to access the available publishing options.

Summary Links

Near the bottom of the default home page you'll find a section for summary links. When you want to add a link, switch to edit mode and click the New Link option under Summary Links. When you choose to add a link, you'll be presented with a New Link dialog that provides you with many options (see Figure 6-5).

Web Parts

Right below the summary links, you'll find some web part zones (see Figure 6-6). As you may have guessed, web part zones are containers for web parts. Adding web parts to your pages is as easy as clicking one of the Add a Web Part links. The various web parts that come with SharePoint Server 2010 are discussed in Chapter 8.

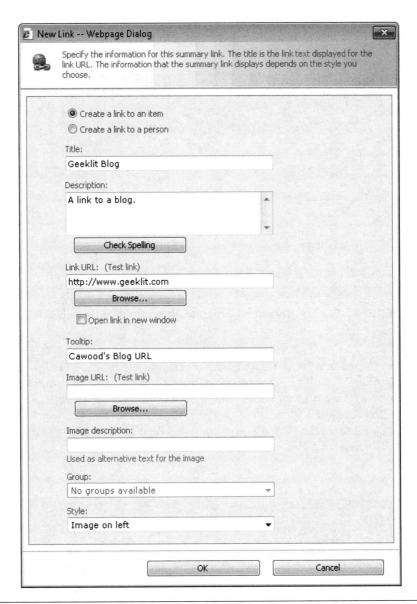

FIGURE 6-5   Adding a new link

Creating Pages and Using Page Layouts

Clearly, you'll need to create your own pages if you want to fully utilize publishing sites. To create a new page, select Site Actions | New Page. You'll be asked to supply the name of the page you want to create. When you click Create, the new page will open. Most likely, the first thing you'll want to do is select the page layout that will be

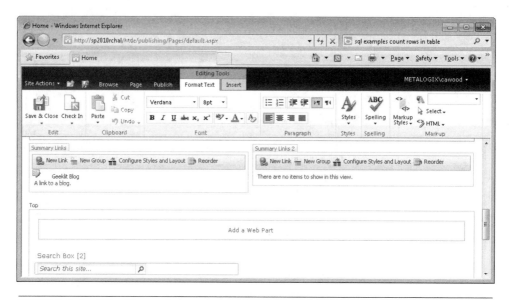

FIGURE 6-6 The Top web part zone after adding a Search Box

used for the new page. Page layouts determine the position of elements on publishing pages, but they also help determine the options available within the page. For example, some page layouts include a prominent image and others do not.

To change the page layout, make sure you have the page in edit mode, then click the Page tab on the ribbon and expand the Page Layout drop-down button to show the available page layouts (see Figure 6-7).

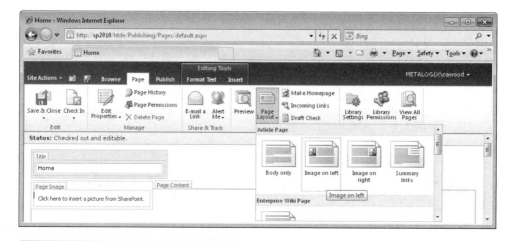

FIGURE 6-7 Applying a page layout to a page

The Pages List

While it's true that you could navigate to each page when you have page tasks to complete, you might also want to be able to apply actions to multiples pages at the same time. Since the pages within a publishing site are stored within a pages list, you can navigate to the list and view the pages in SharePoint's famous list view.

To find the pages list, choose Site Actions | View All Site Content and then scroll down a bit to find the Pages library under the Document Libraries section. Once you have navigated to the Pages library, you'll see the regular list view showing all the pages in the publishing site. If you expand the drop-down menu next to one of the page names, you'll see the options available to you (see Figure 6-8). The options include Check In, Check Out, Discard Check Out, Version History, Manage Permissions, Send To, Compliance Details and Delete. Of course, some options are contextual, so not all of the options will appear in all cases.

Remember that you have the option of selecting multiple pages by clicking the check box next to the items you want to select. You can select all items by checking the box next to the Type column.

Site Actions

Just like the item options, the Site Actions options are also contextual. As you navigate from one type of site to another, you'll find that you see different options. Publishing sites offer these choices:

- **Hide Ribbon** Allows you to hide or show the ribbon for the current page. To try this option, create a subsite based on the Publishing Site template and then open the Site Actions menu of the new site.
- **New Page** Create a new page in the site.

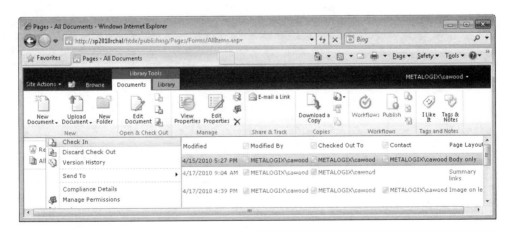

FIGURE 6-8 Selecting the actions menu for a page list item

- **New Document Library** Create a new document library in the site.
- **New Site** Create a new subsite.
- **More Options** Open the Create dialog for sites, pages, lists, and libraries.
- **Manage Content and Structure** Access the task-based Site Content and Structure interface. This interface was discussed in Chapter 2.
- **View All Site Content** View the contents of the current site. If you're trying to find a list, library, or site, this view can be very useful.
- **Edit in SharePoint Designer** Open SharePoint Designer, which allows you to customize various aspects of SharePoint. SharePoint Designer is discussed in Chapter 9.
- **Site Permissions** Manage the users and groups that have rights to the site and exactly which rights they have.
- **Site Settings** Set the options for the current site.

Master Pages

Page layouts are useful, but if you really want to change the look and feel of your site, you need to switch or customize the master page. Master pages define the underlying structure of SharePoint pages.

To change the master page, you'll need to have publishing enabled. Go to Site Actions | Site Settings and, under the Look and Feel section, click Master Page. The Site Master Page Settings page will open and let you customize the master page settings (see Figure 6-9).

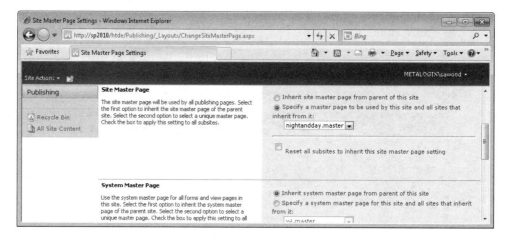

FIGURE 6-9 Setting the master page

Publishing Site with Workflow

If you would like to add some more structure to your publishing experience, you might want to create a publishing site with workflow instead of a regular publishing site. As the name implies, edits under this type of site need to be approved by a user who has sufficient rights.

One thing you'll notice about the Publishing Site with Workflow site template is that you'll have another option in the Publish tab of the ribbon: Schedule. The scheduling feature allows you to set a time frame for publishing the page (see Figure 6-10). You can set both start and end dates for the page to be live.

Publishing Approval

The other options you'll see in the Publish tab are for the content approval workflow. If you are logged in as a user who has permission to edit, but not approve, changes, then you'll find that your edits will not go live until a user with sufficient permissions approves the changes. Of course, it is also possible that your changes can be rejected. Content approval workflow is discussed more in Chapter 3.

Publishing Site Exercise

This quick review exercise will walk you through the process of creating a new SharePoint publishing site and give you a chance to try some of the formatting features available in SharePoint publishing site pages. For this exercise, you'll be creating a publishing site with workflow. At the end of the exercise, you'll have

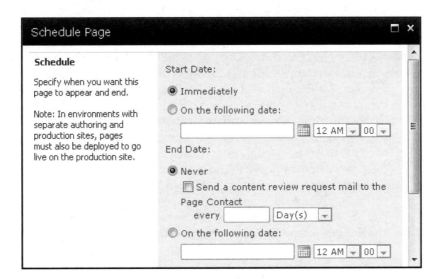

FIGURE 6-10   Setting the start and end dates for a page to be published

FIGURE 6-11 The final result

a publishing site with a home page that looks something like Figure 6-11. The example shown here is a site advertising a company charity drive.

The first thing you'll want to do is create the site and add some content to the main page:

1. Navigate to the site that will be the parent site of the new publishing site.
2. Choose Site Actions | New Site.
3. When the Create dialog opens, choose the Content category.
4. Select Publishing Site with Workflow and enter a name and URL.
5. When the new site has been provisioned, click the Edit button in the ribbon.
6. Now that you're in the site and have the home page open to edit mode, enter some text in the Page Content section. Here you can try some of the formatting features. For example, add a heading line to the top of your page content and use the Markup Styles option in the ribbon to assign the Heading 1 (H1) style. Also, try adding some color and other formatting such as bold and italics. You could also change the name of your home page. For example, in this case, the home page name has been changed to Charity Drive Home.

   Next, you'll add an image to the home page.
7. If you already have your image in SharePoint, you can skip this step. However, if you have not uploaded your home page image yet, you'll need to do that before you can select it. First, make sure you've saved the changes to your home page. You'll find a little Save & Close icon where the Edit button used to be. After you've saved the page, go to Site Actions | View All Site Content. As you saw in previous chapters, this will bring up a listing of everything under the current site. In this case, you'll add your image from your computer to the Images library for the charity site.

8. Under Document Libraries, click Images.
9. Click Add New Item.
10. Click Browse and find your image from your computer, then click OK to add the image to the Images library. Since there is content approval on this site, you may need to choose to check in the image.
11. From the breadcrumb navigation, click the link to the home page of your site. In the example shown, it's called Company Charity Drive.

 You can also navigate to the site's home page by clicking on the site image in the top-left corner of the page. Since you have not changed it yet, it will look like an orange box with three people in it.

12. You should now be back to the site home page. Once again, click Edit to get the home page in edit mode. You are now ready to add your page image, so click the link that reads Click Here to Insert a Picture from SharePoint.
13. Next to Selected Image, click the Browse button and find your image in the Images library. Select your image and click OK. In the Edit Image Properties dialog, you'll find a number of choices, including the alt text that appears when someone hovers over the image and some useful layout options such as the image alignment. Once you've set your options, click OK to add the image to the page.

 If the image is not the right size, you can change how it is displayed by dragging the anchors around the border. This action does not actually resize the original image, but simply changes how it is displayed.

Next, you'll add a new page where you can add directions to the event.

14. As you've seen throughout this book, there are generally multiple methods to complete actions in SharePoint. For example, to create a new page, you could use the Site Actions menu, or you could even navigate to the Pages library and add a new item from there. However, since you're already on the home page, you'll use the wiki-style page creation shortcut. Simply type the name of the page you wish to create in square brackets (for example, [Directions]) and then save the page.
15. Once the page is saved, click the Directions link to create the new page. Once you choose Create, you'll be taken to the new publishing page.
16. At this time, you don't need to make any changes to the Directions page, so click the home page icon or the home page link in the breadcrumb to get back to the main page.

    The final step will publish your new page so that others can enjoy it.
17. Once you're back at the home page, switch to the Publish tab in the ribbon and choose to Publish your page. If you did not have rights to publish, you might only be able to submit the changes for approval by someone who has approval rights on the page. When you elect to publish a page, you'll be asked for a comment so that a history will be maintained of each modification.

Congratulations, you have created your publishing site!

7

My Sites and Personalization

HOW TO...

- Create a My Site
- Use your My Site to share information
- Add a personal blog to your My Site
- Make changes to your SharePoint profile
- Personalize SharePoint pages
- Work with personalization sites

In Chapter 1, you learned that Microsoft CEO Steve Ballmer recently described SharePoint as "a general-purpose platform for connecting people with information." This chapter focuses on the "connecting people" part of that statement by exploring SharePoint My Sites, your personal profile and personalization sites. It's important to remember that My Sites are a SharePoint Server 2010 feature, so you won't get all of the options described in this chapter if you are using the free version—SharePoint Foundation 2010.

My Sites

Many people like to use the analogy that SharePoint My Sites are Microsoft's version of Facebook pages for business. However, as mentioned in Chapter 5, SharePoint My Sites, which were available in SharePoint Portal Server 2003, actually preceded Facebook. Of course, when explaining SharePoint to new users, it's convenient to use the analogy because more people have used Facebook than SharePoint—so far.

Most users don't have rights to create sites—or even lists—on their corporate SharePoint server. This can severely limit your ability to share your files and information and therefore may hinder your connection with other users. My Sites are the solution to this problem—your My Site is where you have control.

Creating Your Own My Site

When SharePoint was installed and your SharePoint server was configured, My Sites were not created for every SharePoint user. Only when you choose to use you're My Site will SharePoint actually provision a site for you. This is one of the ways that SharePoint itself is helping to prevent the dreaded SharePoint sprawl phenomenon. After all, if some people decide to not use their My Sites, then why bother creating one for them?

If you'd like to experiment with your My Site, the first thing you'll need to do is create it. If you look in the top-right corner of a SharePoint page, you'll see your name and a drop-down menu that includes a few useful options. One of the options is My Site—the link that allows you to "Open your personal homepage" (see Figure 7-1). The first time you use this link, your My Site will be created for you.

When you first make it to your My Site, you'll see that there isn't very much there (see Figure 7-2). The reason for this is quite simply that this is your area to do what you want. A framework is provided for you, but you have the freedom to add what you think is most useful.

Naturally, you'll want to add some content to your My Site. To create some lists or upload files to your My Site, click the My Content link at the top of the page. When you do so, SharePoint will show you the message "Please wait while your personal site is setup for the first time and your default document libraries and lists are created. This may take several seconds." While this message is presented, SharePoint is creating elements of your My Site, including a Shared Documents library, a Personal Documents library, and a Shared Pictures library (see Figure 7-3). These libraries allow you to keep some documents private and also share some publicly.

If you want to further organize the content within these libraries, you can create folders and introduce your own filing system. However, if your server is set up with the new Enterprise Metadata Management (EMM) features, you may want to use managed terms to create a taxonomy instead. EMM was discussed in Chapter 5.

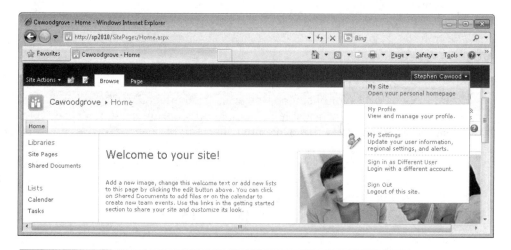

FIGURE 7-1   The link to your My Site

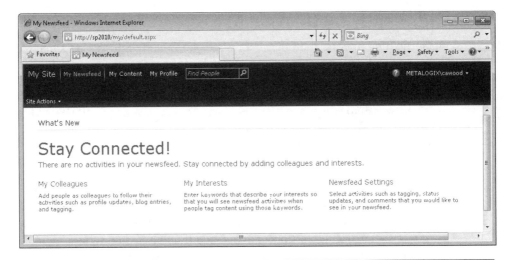

FIGURE 7-2   A brand spanking new My Site

 If you have Microsoft Office installed, you can click the Set as Default My Site link on your My Content page to specify that you'd like Office to remember your My Site URL. This makes it easier for you to use your My Site with Office applications such as Microsoft Outlook. Using SharePoint with client applications is discussed in Chapter 10.

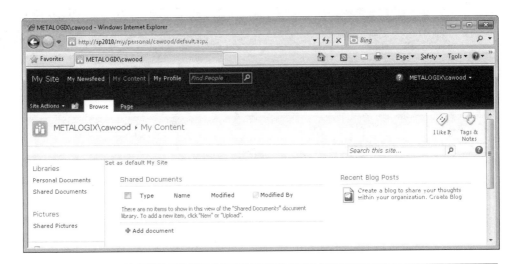

FIGURE 7-3   The My Content page

Adding a Blog to Your My Site

One of the fundamental ingredients in the flavor of a My Site is a personal blog. On the right side of your My Content page, you'll see that there is a control displaying your recent blog posts. Of course, you haven't written any yet, so there won't be any posts showing.

If you switch to edit mode, the web part zones on the page will be displayed and you can see that the blog posts are being displayed via a web part (see Figure 7-4). If you want, you can add and remove web parts from your My Site pages.

Having that empty web part isn't all that useful, so the next step is to create a blog. Under the text that reads, "Create a blog to share your thoughts within your organization," you'll see a Create Blog link. Click this link and a blog site will be provisioned for you (see Figure 7-5). Blog sites were discussed in Chapter 5.

At this point, you may be wondering what else was included with your new My Site. If you switch to the My Content page and then go to Site Actions | View All Site Content, you'll be able to see the libraries that were created. The list includes Customized Reports, Form Templates, Personal Documents, Shared Documents, Style Library, and Shared Pictures. If you created a blog, you'll also see a site called Blog under the Sites and Workspaces section. These libraries are meant to get you started, but don't let them restrain your creativity; go to Site Actions | More Options to see what you can create.

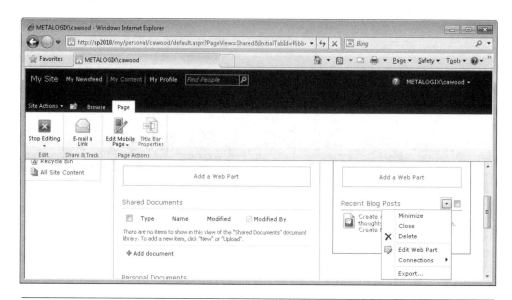

FIGURE 7-4 The My Content page in edit mode

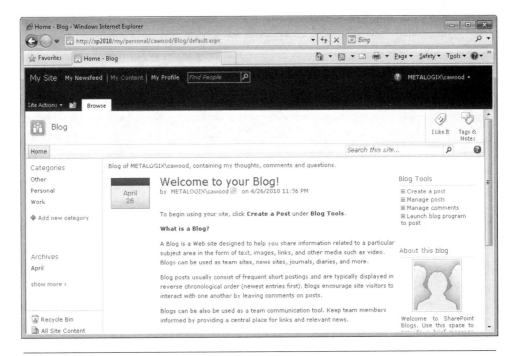

FIGURE 7-5   A new blog under a My Site

Viewing Your Newsfeed

In addition to the My Content link, at the top of your My Site home page, you'll see a My Newsfeed link. The newsfeed will show your recent activity on the server. For example, you learned in Chapter 5 that your tagging activities will be shown in your newsfeed. You'll also see three sections on this page: My Colleagues, My Interests, and Newsfeed Settings.

My Colleagues allows you to add people to your personal list of colleagues (see Figure 7-6). My Interests takes you to the Interests section of your profile settings and gives you the option of specifying your areas of expertise so that others who are looking for subject matter experts can find you. Newsfeed Settings takes you to the Activities I Am Following section of your profile—which just happens to be the next topic in this chapter.

 Tip   Since a user's profile is only created when that user logs into SharePoint for the first time, you will not be able to add users who have not logged into the system.

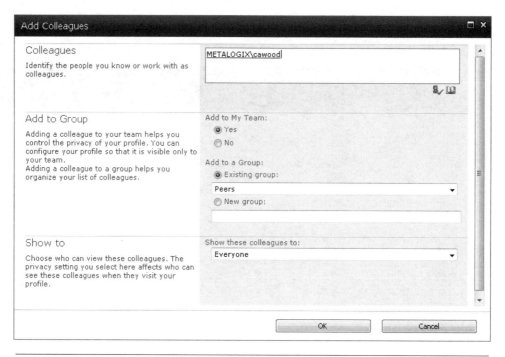

FIGURE 7-6 Adding a colleague to the My Colleagues section

Your SharePoint Profile

Your SharePoint profile allows you to provide useful information about yourself. From the My Profile page, you can click the Edit My Profile link under your picture to access your profile settings. The profile includes data such as Basic Information, Contact Information, Details, and Newsfeed Settings. For example, you can make your presence more personal by adding a photo to your profile. To do so, simply edit your profile and, under the Basic Information section, click the Choose Picture button. When you upload an image from your computer, it will be added to your SharePoint profile (see Figure 7-7).

After adding a picture, you'll see it shown in many places, but your profile page is one good example (see Figure 7-8). Microsoft clearly believes that this feature will be used by very large organizations, because the text under the Choose Picture option reads, "Upload a picture to help others easily recognize you at meetings and events."

An interesting aspect of the profile page that should not be overlooked is that you can customize your profile page for different people. At the top of the profile page, there is a drop-down menu next to the text "View My Profile as seen by" (see Figure 7-9). This allows you to select different users and then customize your profile for that user. For example, you might want to show a web part containing your current tasks list to your manager, but not to the rest of your team.

FIGURE 7-7   Adding a profile image

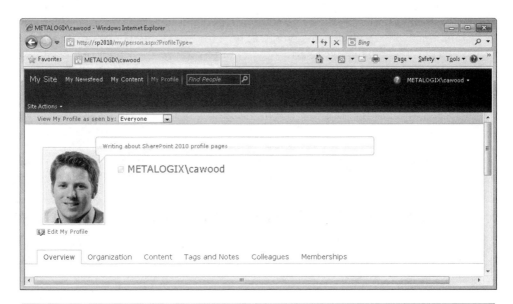

FIGURE 7-8   The profile page after adding a personal image

FIGURE 7-9 The personalized view drop-down menu for the profile page

Personalizing SharePoint Pages

Although your My Site is the area that you'll probably customize the most, it isn't the only personalization option in SharePoint. In fact, if you have rights to do so, many pages will allow you to personalize the look of the page just for you. In other words, an administrator could customize a page for all users, but you can also choose to personalize pages as an end user, to tune the content you want to see. For example, there may be a web part that you will never need. Using the personalization option, you can remove that web part from the page and use the screen real estate for something more important. Similarly, if there is something that you want to see on the page, you may choose to add a web part.

To personalize a page, click the drop-down arrow in the top-right corner of the page and select the Personalize This Page option (see Figure 7-10).

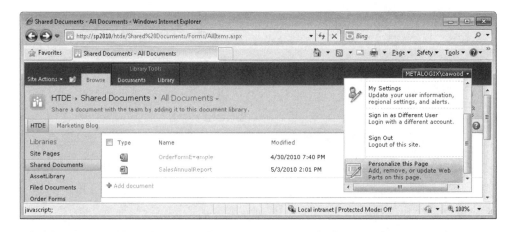

FIGURE 7-10 The page personalization option

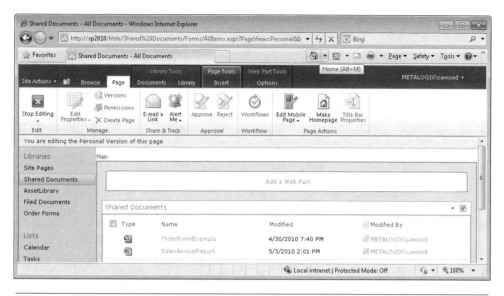

FIGURE 7-11   Personalizing a page

When you choose to personalize a page, the page will switch to edit mode (see Figure 7-11), but with a very important difference from the regular editing option—any changes you make will only be applied to your view of the page. If another user visits the page, she will not see the changes you have made.

The personalization option is useful because it allows end users to make pages their own. Once you have the page in edit mode, you have the option of making changes, such as adding or removing web parts, but you don't need to worry about how your customizations will affect other SharePoint users.

 The personalization isn't available when the "Wiki Page Home Page" site feature is activated.

Personalization Sites

The first thing to note about personalization sites is that they are not the same as My Sites. Personalization sites are generally used by SharePoint administrators to provide content that is specific to individual users. In other words, your My Site is the place where you can share information about yourself, add your own content, and possibly create your own lists and subsites. Personalization sites are created by SharePoint administrators to show users content that is dynamically presented just for them. For example, if your organization developed a paycheck web part, the personalization site would change the data displayed based on who is viewing the page. To make it easier for people to use the page, the administrator can add a link to the personalization site on each user's My Site.

If that description isn't enough, you'll get a little bit of help from SharePoint as well. When you create a personalization site, the following text appears on the home page:

> Personalization sites are designed to help you provide an uncompromised distinct personalization experience that connects your portal to users' My Sites. Use this site to push personalized and targeted information to your users based on who they are and why they visit your portal. The personalization site template helps you identify the current user and use their profile to accurately target and present information that is specific to that user and his or her needs. This gives you the opportunity to offer a me centric view of your portal to your users.
>
> As an example you can use a personalization site to unlock information buried in various business systems and by your site structure, to provide a one stop shop experience that easily allows users to view and access information they need to perform their job or task. Or you could offer an experience which helps to better align your organization with its goals, by using your personalization site to drive user behavior through performance indicators and metrics, which can be specifically set for an individual user based on their role.
>
> After your personalization site is developed, to make your personalization site a permanent location on your users' My Site navigation bar, contact your administrator to register your personalization site.

Since personalization sites are meant to be the starting point for your own custom needs, a new personalization site comes with very little out of the box. If you browse the All Site Content page, you'll see that no lists, libraries, or subsites are created. However, there are a couple of important ingredients added to this flavor of site. If you switch the home page to edit mode, you'll see that the web part page comes with two filters: the Current User Filter and the Profile Property Filter (see Figure 7-12). These filters provide the option of filtering content based on who is viewing it or filtering properties within each person's profile, respectively.

My Sites, SharePoint profiles, and personalization sites are all key factors in adding a folksy feeling to a SharePoint server. They also provide a valuable social networking aspect that can be used to ease the sharing and discovery of information across your enterprise. As a former Microsoft employee, I understand just how valuable My Sites can be to a large company. If I was looking for information about a particular Microsoft project, I could search for users who worked on that project and then visit their My Sites to get the most up-to-date information. Search engines are certainly useful, but getting the right information at the right time from the right person is invaluable.

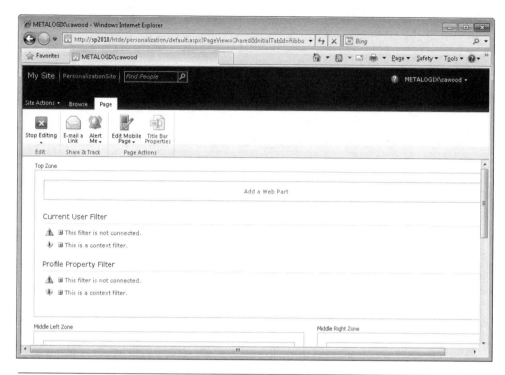

FIGURE 7-12   The personalization site home page in edit mode

8

Web Parts

HOW TO...

- Add web parts to a page
- Customize web parts
- Use the out-of-the-box web parts

Web parts are flexible pieces of functionality that can be added to pages when they are needed. For example, if you want to show the contents of a list that's located in some other part of the site, you don't need to ask your users to click a link to see the data; instead, you can add a web part to your page that displays the data. Want to show your Microsoft Outlook calendar within SharePoint? You can use the My Calendar web part to do just that.

The good news is that the Enterprise version of SharePoint Server 2010 comes with roughly 70 web parts. SharePoint Foundation provides a subset of the list. However, the downside of that impressive number is that there aren't enough pages in this book to discuss all of them. This chapter gives you a reference list and highlights some examples for you to try.

Adding Web Parts to a Page

If you want to experiment with web parts, the first thing you'll need is a web part page. To create a new page, choose Site Actions | More Options. Once the Create dialog is open, choose the Page type and then select Web Part Page. Next, click Create, give your page a name, and choose a layout.

 Tip Your site home page (that is, the default.aspx page) can also contain web parts.

159

You'll notice that different layouts will allow you to present your web parts in various columns. The default option is Header, Footer, and three Columns. This essentially means that you'll have one wide zone, then three columns containing a zone each, and then another wide zone at the bottom (see Figure 8-1). If you don't use a zone, it will collapse and the screen real estate will be used by the other zones. This means that choosing a layout with lots of zones might be the best choice if you might need to make changes to the page in the future.

Note Under the Create options, you can also choose a location in which to create the page. The default is the Site Assets list, but you might want to put your page somewhere else.

Once you click Create, SharePoint creates the new web part page for you. In edit mode, you'll be able to see the zones defined by the page layout, but if you click Stop Editing, you'll see that the new page is completely blank.

To begin adding web parts, you'll need to be in edit mode, so if you're not in edit mode already, click the Edit Page button in the Edit section of the ribbon. Once in edit mode, you can click any of the Add a Web Part links you see on the page. You'll be able to choose the target web part zone after you make your selection. However, the link that you click will determine which zone is selected as the default for the add operation, so you may want to click the correct link rather than changing the zone later.

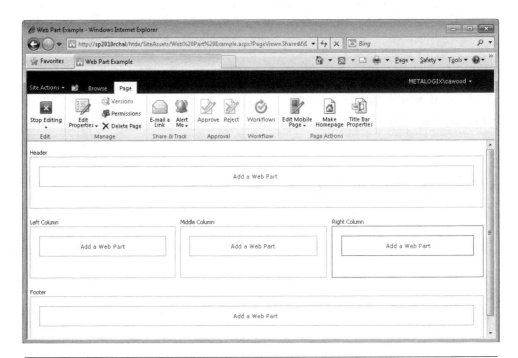

FIGURE 8-1 A new web part page

Note You might notice that some of the names of your lists appear in the web part gallery. This is because some web parts are created specifically to show list content (for example, Picture Libraries). If you have those types of lists in your site, you'll be able to use them with these web parts without having to do any configuration. Simply add the web part, and the data from your list will appear.

After clicking Add a Web Part, a list of the web parts available on your server will appear at the top of the page. You'll still be able to see your page at the bottom. This allows you to choose the web parts you want and still have the context of the page you're editing (see Figure 8-2).

For this exercise, choose the Table Of Contents web part from the Content Rollup category. If you are using SharePoint Foundation, you won't have this web part, so simply choose another. Once you have made your selection, choose the target zone for the new web part. Since the layout has defined the width of each web part zone, you'll want to add your web parts to zones that best fit their real estate needs on your page. For example, a web part that needs to be wide would fit best in the Header or Footer zone of the default page layout. If you want to use a narrower space for your part, then you'd choose one of the three narrow columns. After you add the Table Of Contents web part, you'll see that it will show links to the sites and lists under your site (see Figure 8-3).

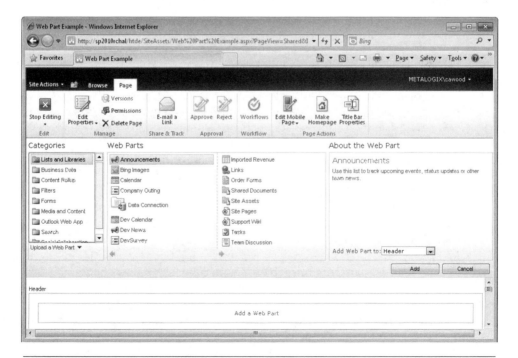

FIGURE 8-2   Adding a web part

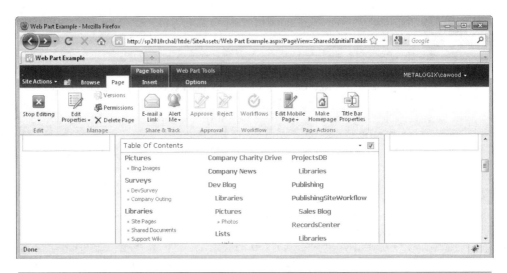

FIGURE 8-3 The Table Of Contents web part showing links

 Tip Technically, the width of the zones in the page layout only becomes a factor when multiple web parts have been added to the page. If no web parts are in a zone, then that space can be used by web parts in other zones.

After adding a web part, you'll have the option to set various settings that control how that web part will behave. This allows you to customize the web part to suit your particular needs. Of course, different web parts will have different settings, but thanks to their shared architecture, you'll be able to get to those settings the same way.

To open the options for the Table Of Contents web part, make sure you have your page in edit mode and then expand the drop-down menu next to the heading of the web part. Once there, choose Edit Web Part from the options (see Figure 8-4).

The web part options panel will open on the right side of the page. Inside, you'll find the options neatly arranged into categories so that you can find them with ease. For example, if you wanted to change the width or height of the web part, you'd expand the Appearance section (see Figure 8-5).

Other options for the Table Of Contents web part include specifying the level of your site hierarchy to start the table, how many levels to show, and whether pages should be included or hidden. The Layout and Advanced sections are generally used for settings that are available for all web parts—for example, whether users are allowed to close the web part, minimize it, or hide it. Some users may choose to hide a web part if it is taking up room that they'd rather see used by other elements on the page.

This section covered the process of creating a web part page, adding web parts, and setting options to customize web parts to your needs. The rest of this chapter is a reference for the out-of-the-box web parts that come with SharePoint Server 2010. If you are using SharePoint Foundation 2010, or your server does not have all the features enabled, you will see a subset of this list.

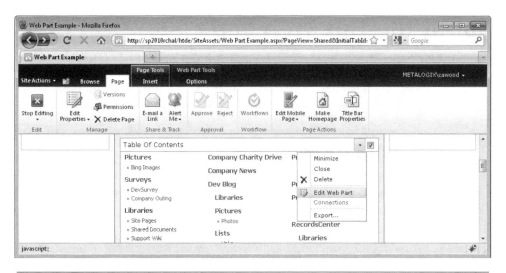

FIGURE 8-4   The web part actions menu

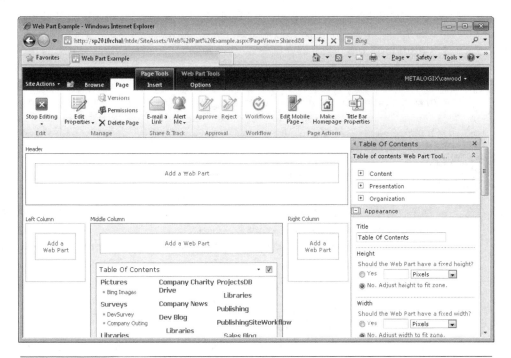

FIGURE 8-5   The web part settings

Out-of-the-Box Web Parts

As previously mentioned, over 70 web parts ship with the Enterprise version of SharePoint Server 2010, and a subset of those are available in SharePoint Foundation 2010. This reference section lists the web parts and provides a bit more detail than the descriptions you'll see in the SharePoint interface for adding web parts.

Lists and Libraries

Most of these web parts are self-explanatory. Functionality such as announcements, links, tasks, and calendars can be found in lists as well, but a web part will be a better choice at times.

- **Announcements** *Use this list to track upcoming events, status updates, or other team news.*

  This is probably one of the more commonly used web parts. Of all the content on a SharePoint server, announcements are likely the items that you'd least want to have lost in the shuffle of everything else. The Announcements web part keeps that from happening. Add it to any page and you'll be able to ensure that the news is visible from different areas of the server. Announcement lists were discussed in Chapter 4.

- **Calendar** *Use the Calendar list to keep informed of upcoming meetings, deadlines, and other important events.*

  Add a Calendar web part and help your team keep on schedule. You'll find that this calendar offers a number of convenient features such as the ability to attach files to events, maintain a version history, and view the calendar with your own custom views (see Figure 8-6).

 Calendar lists were discussed in Chapter 4.

- **Data Connection** *Used by the Business Connectivity Services features that allow a connection to data sources external to SharePoint.*
- **Links** *Use the links list for links to Web pages that your team members will find interesting or useful.*
- **Tasks** *Use the Tasks list to keep track of work that you or your team needs to complete.*
- **Team Discussion** *Use the Team Discussion list to hold newsgroup-style discussions on topics relevant to your team.*

  This web part allows you to show off the latest discussion board entries on any page. One problem with collaboration features is that the "out of sight, out of mind" principle can be particularly apropos. If users don't actually navigate to your discussion lists, the content could end up buried, but if the latest discussion board topics are on the home page, they are more likely to be seen.

FIGURE 8-6   A Calendar web part in monthly view

Business Data

The web parts in this section help fulfill SharePoint's original mandate of being a portal to your company data. This category of web parts provides a vast array of tools for connecting to data sources and presenting the data in useful ways.

SharePoint may be used for many types of data storage today, but in the past, the same types of data would have been stored in an innumerable range of other systems. Rather than moving the data into SharePoint, your organization may have decided to leave that data where it is and then use the business data web parts in SharePoint 2010 to surface the information to the end user.

- **Business Data Actions**   *Displays a list of actions from Business Data Connectivity.*
- **Business Data Connectivity Filter**   *Filters the contents of Web Parts using a list of values from Business Data Connectivity.*

- **Business Data Item**   *Displays one item from a data source in Business Data Connectivity.*
- **Business Data Item Builder**   *Creates a Business Data item from parameters in the query string and provides it to other Web Parts.*
- **Business Data List**   *Displays a list of items from a data source in Business Data Connectivity.*
- **Business Data Related List**   *Displays a list of items related to one or more parent items from a data source in Business Data Connectivity.*
- **Chart Web Part**   *Helps you to visualize your data on SharePoint sites and portals.*

  The SharePoint 2010 Chart web part boasts some useful functionality. When you try it out, you'll find lots of options for data connections and display. If you want, you can run the Chart web part wizard, which enables you to connect the Chart web part to an existing list. Anytime you need a dynamic graphic, you can try this web part (see Figure 8-7).

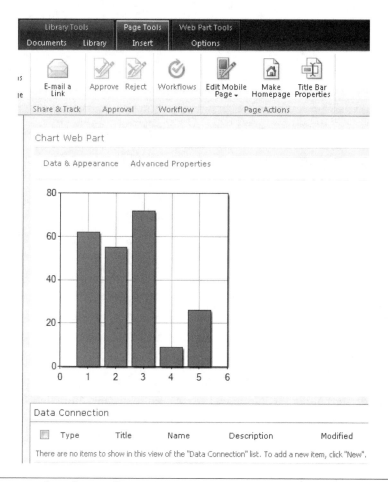

FIGURE 8-7   The Chart web part

These web parts are added with the Enterprise edition:

- **Excel Web Access**   *Use the Excel Web Access Web Part to interact with an Excel workbook as a web page.*
- **Indicator Details**   *Displays the details of a single Status Indicator. Status Indicators display an important measure for an organization and may be obtained from other data sources, including SharePoint lists, Excel workbooks, and SQL Server 2005 Analysis Services KPIs.*
- **Status List**   *Shows a list of Status Indicators. Status Indicators display important measures for your organization, and show how your organization is performing with respect to your goals.*
- **Visio Web Access**   *Enables viewing and refreshing of Visio Web Drawings.*

Content Rollup

This category of web parts is highly popular because it allows you to reuse your content in different sections of your server. This allows you to maintain one authoritative store of the data but, at the same time, display the data in different pages.

- **Categories**   *Displays categories from the Site Directory.*
- **Content Query**   *Displays a dynamic view of content from your site.*

  The Content Query web part is an easy way to display content from another part of the site. For example, you can configure the setting to show the content of a particular list (see Figure 8-8). After you choose a list and save your changes, the web part will dynamically update every time there is a change to the source list (see Figure 8-9).

- **Relevant Documents**   *Displays documents that are relevant to the current user.*
- **RSS Viewer**   *Displays an RSS feed.*
- **Site Aggregator**   *Displays sites of your choice.*
- **Sites in Category**   *Displays sites from the Site Directory within a specific category.*
- **Summary Links**   *Allows authors to create links that can be grouped and styled.*
- **Table Of Contents**   *Displays the navigation hierarchy of your site.*

  The Table Of Contents web part was discussed earlier in this chapter.

- **Web Analytics Web Part**   *Displays the most viewed content, most frequent search queries from a site, or most frequent search queries from a search center.*
- **WSRP Viewer**   *Displays portlets from web sites using Web Services for Remote Portlets 1.1.*

  For more information about web services for remote portlets, you can read this article:http://en.wikipedia.org/wiki/Web_Services_for_Remote_Portlets.

- **XML Viewer**   *Transforms XML data using XSL and shows the results.*

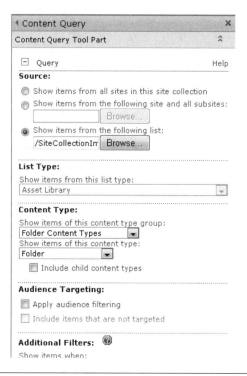

FIGURE 8-8   Options for the Content Query web part

Filters

Filter web parts are included with the Enterprise features. They give you the option of offering your users a quick way to customize the result set in another web part. For example, if you have a list showing the contents of an Announcements list on your page, you can add the ability to filter which announcements are displayed based on the values in one of the columns in the list.

 The filter web parts will not work with every type of web part, so you'll need to investigate whether your scenario is supported. The web parts that are supported will appear in the list of possible connections once you add a filter web part to the page.

- **Choice Filter**   *Filters the contents of Web Parts using a list of values entered by the page author.*
- **Current User Filter**   *Filters the contents of Web Parts by using properties of the current user.*
- **Date Filter**   *Filter the contents of Web Parts by allowing users to enter or pick a date.*
- **Filter Actions**   *Use the Filter Actions Web Part when you have two or more filter Web Parts on one Web Part Page and you want to synchronize the display of the filter results.*

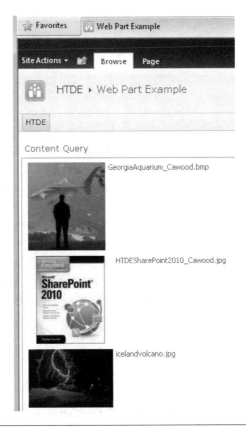

FIGURE 8-9   A Content Query web part showing the contents of a picture library

- **Page Field Filter**   *Filters the contents of Web Parts using information about the current page.*
- **Query String (URL) Filter**   *Filters the contents of Web Parts using values passed via the query string.*
- **SharePoint List Filter**   *Filters the contents of Web Parts by using a list of values.*
- **SQL Server Analysis Services Filter**   *Filters the contents of Web Parts using a list of values from SQL Server Analysis Services cubes.*
- **Text Filter**   *Filters the contents of Web Parts by allowing users to enter a text value.*

The Text Filter web part provides the option of filtering other web part data based on the text within a particular column—such as the Title. Once you've added this web part to your page, you'll need to connect it to another web part on the same page. To do this, go to the right of the web part heading and find the web part drop-down menu. Choose Connections and then Send Filter Values To. This will expand a menu of the web parts on the page that support the Text Filter web part (see Figure 8-10). If you have thousands of items in your list, this type of filtering can save a substantial amount of time.

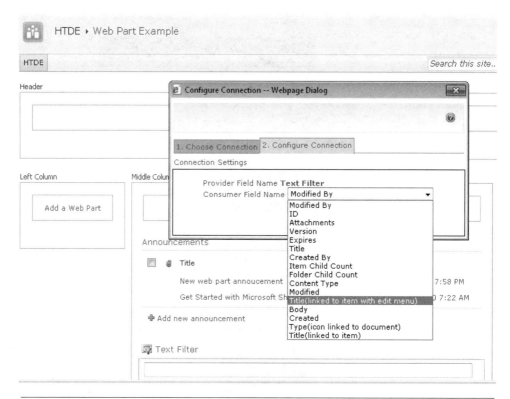

FIGURE 8-10 Connecting the Text Filter web part

In this example, an Announcements list is being filtered by the Modified date value (see Figure 8-11). Only the announcements with the specified filter value are being displayed.

 The Text Filter web part filters by the entire string. For example, if you connected to an Announcements list by the Title and wanted to find an announcement called "Intranet is live," you would need to type the whole title.

Forms

The web parts in this category have highly specialized functions. The HTML Form web part allows you to filter the contents of other web parts using HTML form elements such as a check box or a drop-down box, and the InfoPath Form web part is used only to display forms that were created using Microsoft InfoPath.

- **HTML Form Web Part** *Connects simple form controls to other Web Parts.*
- **InfoPath Form Web Part** *Use to display an InfoPath browser-enabled form.*

Microsoft InfoPath form libraries are discussed in Chapter 10.

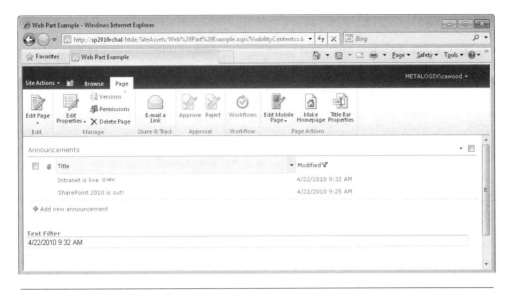

FIGURE 8-11   A text filter applied to an Announcements list

Media and Content

These web parts add flexibility to your content options. For example, the Content Editor web part allows you to add any HTML-formatted content you want—you can use it to add your own custom HTML, including adding Adobe Flash content. Other web parts in this category make it easy to liven up your SharePoint pages with media such as images and video.

- **Content Editor**   *Allows authors to enter rich text content.*
- **Image Viewer**   *Displays a specified image.*
- **Media Web Part**   *Use to embed media clips (video and audio) in a web page.*
  As you would expect, the Media web part allows you to easily show media. For example, you can choose a video from outside of SharePoint if you want—you don't have to store your videos in SharePoint. You can even insert videos into SharePoint wikis.
- **Page Viewer**   *Displays another Web page on this Web page. The other Web page is presented in an IFrame.*
- **Picture Library Slideshow Web Part**   *Use to display a slideshow of images and photos from a picture library.*
  In the previous version of SharePoint, this web part was called This Week in Pictures, but it didn't have anything to do with dates, so it has rightly been renamed. This web part has also been enhanced for 2010. For example, you will find that you have more display options. Picture libraries are discussed in more detail in Chapter 11.
- **Silverlight Web Part**   *A web part to display a Silverlight application.*

Outlook Web App

Outlook Web Access (OWA) is the web-based interface to Microsoft Exchange Server. Many organizations use both Exchange and SharePoint, so having a way to capitalize on the synergy between the two is a slam dunk for web part offerings. If you have access to an OWA-enabled Exchange server, you'll be able to use these parts.

These web parts are most useful in your My Site pages because you need to specify which mailbox you're connecting to, and most users will not have rights to see your mailbox. Although, if you were using a shared mailbox, such as for customer support, you may want other users to have access.

 To configure your web part, you'll need an e-mail alias and the URL for an OWA-enabled Exchange server. Check with your administrator if you don't know the correct URL to use.

- **My Calendar** *Displays your calendar using Outlook Web Access for Microsoft Exchange Server 2003 or later.*
- **My Contacts** *Displays your contacts using Outlook Web Access for Microsoft Exchange Server 2003 or later.*
- **My Inbox** *Displays your inbox using Outlook Web Access for Microsoft Exchange Server 2003 or later.*
- **My Mail Folder** *Displays your mail folder using Outlook Web Access for Microsoft Exchange Server 2000.*

    This OWA web part allows you to specify one of the folders under your mailbox to display in SharePoint (see Figure 8-12).

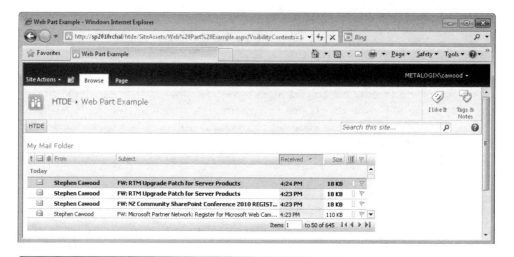

FIGURE 8-12   Displaying the contents of an OWA folder

To use these web parts, you may need to add the SharePoint URL or the OWA URL to your sites list under the Internet Explorer privacy settings. To get there, go to Tools | Internet Options | Security and then add the URL to Trusted Sites or Local Intranet.

- **My Tasks**   *Displays your tasks using Outlook Web Access for Microsoft Exchange Server 2003 or later.*

Search

Search is one of those features that requires no explanation. Sure, most of us don't have to index as many pages as Bing.com, but SharePoint is primarily targeted at large companies, and large companies have lots of data. These web parts will help you make the most of search.

- **Advanced Search Box**   *Displays parameterized search options based on properties and combinations of words.*

  As you have seen in the screenshots in this book and on your own SharePoint server, a basic search box is found in the top-right corner of most pages. However, if you want to beef up the search experience, you can add the Advanced Search Box web part. For example, you can search by the data in a particular column (see Figure 8-13).

 Creating a Search Center Site (basic or enterprise) creates a site and dashboard that utilizes many of these web parts.

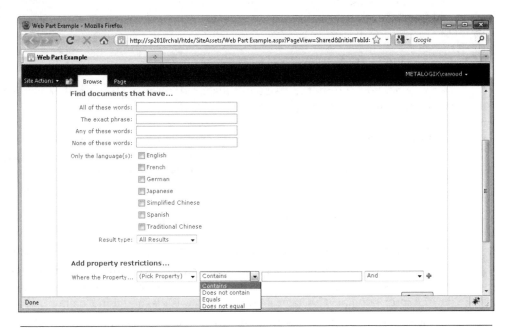

FIGURE 8-13   Setting the properties of a search web part

- **Dual Chinese Search** *Used to search Dual Chinese document and items at the same time.*
- **Federated Results** *Displays search results from a configured location.*
- **People Refinement Panel** *Helps the users to refine people search results.*
- **People Search Box** *Presents a search box that allows users to search for people.*
- **People Search Core Results** *Displays the people search results and the properties associated with them.*
- **Refinement Panel** *Helps the users to refine search results.*
- **Related Queries** *Displays related queries to a user query.*
- **Search Action Links** *Displays the search action links on the search results page.*
- **Search Best Bets** *Displays high-confidence results on a search results page.*

 SharePoint Best Bets are used to help people searching your SharePoint server. For example, if someone searches for something to do with sports (for example, "Water Polo"), you could present a list of options, links, or even a custom message ("Are you looking for the Water Polo league schedule? It can be found here..."). The Best Bets are defined in SharePoint Central Administration.

- **Search Box** *Displays a search box that allows users to search for information.*
- **Search Core Results** *Displays the search results and the properties associated with them.*
- **Search Paging** *Displays links for navigating pages containing search results.*
- **Search Statistics** *Displays the search statistics such as the number of results shown on the current page, total number of results, and time taken to perform the search.*
- **Search Summary** *Displays suggestions for current search query.*
- **Search Visual Best Bet** *Displays Visual Best Bet.*
- **Top Federated Results** *Displays the Top Federated result from the configured location.*

Social Collaboration

I know what you're thinking...isn't all collaboration social? Well, be that as it may, this is the final category of web parts.

- **Contact Details** *Displays details about a contact for this page or site.*
- **Note Board** *Enable users to leave short, publicly viewable notes about this page.*
- **Organization Browser** *This web part displays each person in the reporting chain in an interactive view optimized for browsing organization charts. It is commonly used on My Sites.*
- **Site Users** *Use the Site Users web part to see a list of the site users and their online status.*
- **Tag Cloud** *Displays the most popular subjects being tagged inside your organization.* The Tag Cloud web part is new in SharePoint Server 2010. It's a user-friendly way to see the tags that have been used in SharePoint and quickly tell which are the most popular. The Tag Cloud web part was discussed in Chapter 5.
- **User Tasks** *Displays tasks that are assigned to the current user.*

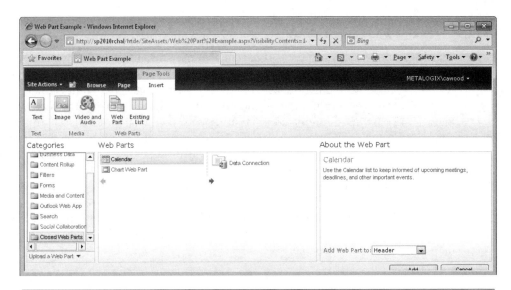

FIGURE 8-14   The Closed Web Parts category

Closed Web Parts

Sometimes when you look at the bottom of the web part categories, you'll see an extra category called Closed Web Parts. This category contains web parts that were added to the page but were subsequently closed using the web part actions drop-down menu.

When a web part is closed, the change is applied to all users, so if you close a web part, you are hiding it from everyone. This might be useful if the web part wasn't behaving properly and your administrator wanted to keep it out of view until the issue is resolved.

To add a web part that has been closed, choose to Edit the page, then go to the Inset tab on the ribbon and choose Web Part—just as if you wanted to add a new web part (see Figure 8-14).

Data View Web Part

The Data View web part allows you to choose how you want to display information from SharePoint. It is arguably the most versatile of web parts. However, to use it you'll need to install the free Microsoft SharePoint Designer client.

Working with the Data View web part is more of a SharePoint Designer or Developer task than an end-user function, so it falls outside the scope of this book. However, there are lots of resources online that will help you learn about this powerful tool. For example, the site www.endusersharepoint.com has published articles about the Data View web part.

Custom Web Parts

SharePoint developers can create custom web parts to fulfill an unlimited number of feature requirements. For example, at a recent SharePoint Saturday conference in New York, I used a population simulation web part called SharePoint Game of Life to demonstrate programming with the new SharePoint 2010 taxonomy features (see Figure 8-15). If you're interested in creating your own web parts, search around and you'll find some useful tutorials online. For example, check out my blog post about developing SharePoint 2010 visual web parts: http://geeklit.blogspot.com/2009/12/sharepoint-2010-visual-web-parts.html.

Writing your own web parts is certainly an option. However, as you've seen in this chapter, roughly 70 web parts come with SharePoint 2010. Be sure to investigate what's available before you or other developers in your company start writing anything new. Although it's true that custom web parts can't do everything you want, they are incredibly useful and flexible.

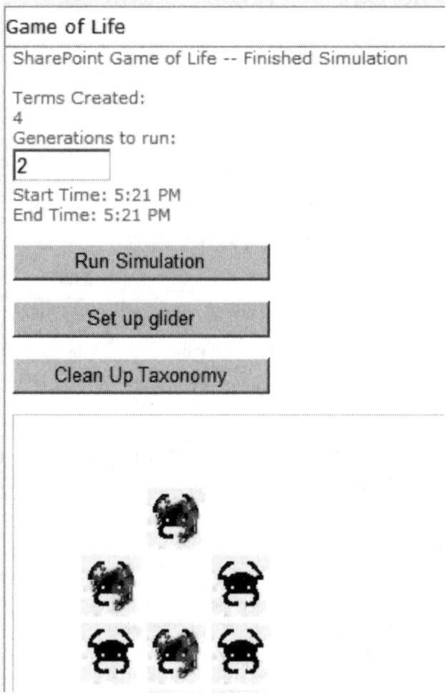

FIGURE 8-15 The SharePoint Game of Life web part

9

Customization

SharePoint is a flexible system, and a large part of that flexibility is that you can implement considerable customization without having to do any development. Without a doubt, there is no one-size-fits-all enterprise information management system that comes out of the box exactly the way that every organization would like. This chapter explores some of the many ways that you can tailor SharePoint to your needs.

List Customizations

SharePoint lists have been discussed in many parts of this book, but one aspect that hasn't been explored thoroughly is how to tweak and mold lists to suit your personal or business requirements. This is one of the most widely used customization options in SharePoint, so it seems fitting that the first topic on the customization list should be list customization.

Custom Lists

Although SharePoint Foundation 2010 includes many list templates out of the box and SharePoint Server 2010 includes even more, the solution to meeting SharePoint customers' needs is not to try and anticipate everything that they might require; the answer is to provide flexible and user-friendly customization options.

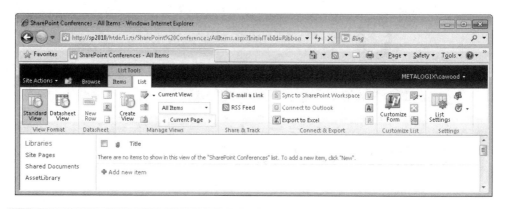

FIGURE 9-1 A new custom list

Imagine that you're working in the marketing department of your company and one of your tasks is to organize your company presence at trade shows. To store the various data you need to track, you decide that you'll use a SharePoint list. The only problem is that there is no out-of-the-box list template that includes a column for information such as the Twitter tag for each event or the sponsorship level for your company at each show. To store this specialized information, you may decide to create your own list or customize an existing list type.

The options for creating lists have been discussed already. The two quickest choices are in the Site Actions menu: More Options, or View All Site Content and then the Create link. To begin this exercise, in the Create dialog, choose to create a custom list. When SharePoint has created the list, you'll see that it comes with one visible column: Title (see Figure 9-1). You need to add more columns to contain your data.

The first step is to click the List tab on the ribbon and then click the Create Column button (see Figure 9-2). This opens the Create Column dialog and allows you to specify exactly what type of column you would like to add.

FIGURE 9-2 The Create Column option in the ribbon

In this first example, you want to add a column to contain the Twitter hashtag for the conference, so choose a single line of text as the data type (see Figure 9-3). Twitter hashtags allow Twitter users to search for tweets that are related to a particular subject. In this way, people who are interested in, for example, one of the conferences can simply search for the hashtag and filter out all the noisy tweets out there about what people are having for lunch and what amazing tricks their pets have performed.

If you scroll down the Create Column dialog to the Additional Column Settings section, you'll see that there are also some other options, such as Add to Default View, which will make the new column visible within the default view. Since Twitter hashtags must be unique to be useful, select Yes for the Enforce Unique Values option (see Figure 9-4). When you choose this option, SharePoint asks you to index the column. Indexing is generally done as a means to make searching faster, but in this example it also serves the purpose of providing a unique Twitter hashtag.

Now that you've added your new column, you can see it in action by clicking the Add New Item link in your custom list. Instead of just asking for a Title, the New Item dialog will now also ask for a Twitter Tag (see Figure 9-5). Because you chose to provide one line of text, that's all your users will be able to enter. Twitter hash tags begin with the hash symbol, but since the default content for this field was set to #, your users will not need to type the hash symbol each time. Furthermore, the list will enforce that each value in this column is unique.

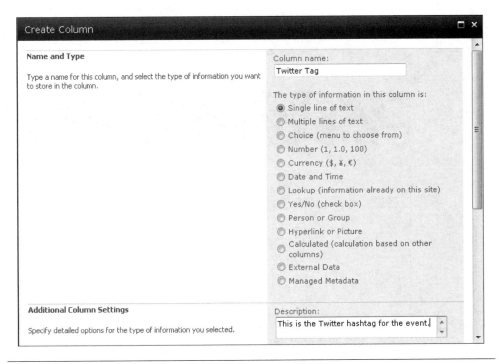

FIGURE 9-3   Specifying the data type for a new column

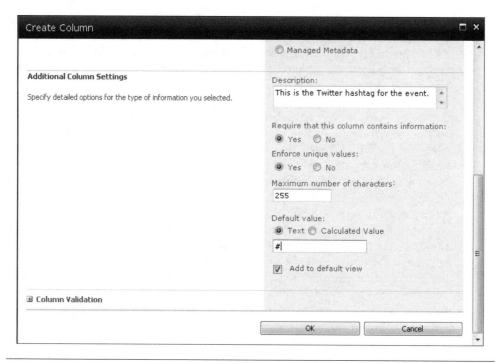

FIGURE 9-4   Setting properties for the new column

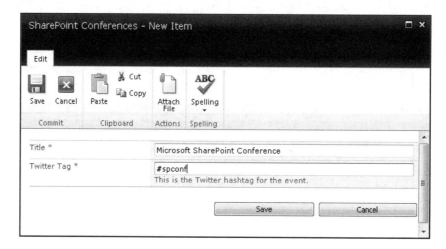

FIGURE 9-5   Adding a new item to the list

Of course, using the Custom List type means that you'll need to add almost all the columns yourself. If there is an existing list that's similar to what you want, you might find that just augmenting the existing list is a faster way to go. However, you should keep in mind that some types of lists have other built-in functionality that you may or may not want to use. For example, calendar, task, contact, and discussion board lists are all able to connect to Microsoft Outlook.

Custom List Example: Mileage Tracker

In this exercise, you'll build on what you've already learned and create an entirely new list from scratch. The list that you'll build in this example enables a real-world scenario: a means of tracking mileage. In fact, this book's technical editor, Sean Wallbridge, uses a list just like this at itgroove (www.itgroove.net).

The Mileage Tracker list will allow employees to easily track how many miles they have driven for work purposes and make it easy for them to produce mileage reports for use in their expense reports. The goal is to enable them to track the reason for each trip, the client account, the date of the trip, and the odometer readings at the beginning and end of the journey. The odometer readings will be used to calculate and store the total mileage for each entry.

The first step is to create a new custom list. To do this, navigate to the site where you want the list to be created and then choose one of the methods mentioned already to create the list.

Once you have a list, you need to add some columns, but first choose List Settings from the List section of the ribbon, scroll down to the list of columns, and click Title to edit the column settings. Change the name of this column to "Reason for trip" and add the description "Please provide a brief description of your trip." Once you have edited the column, save your changes.

Next, create the following columns. To ensure that employees are guided toward proper record keeping, in the Create Column dialog, set all of these columns to require data. This prevents an employee from saving a new entry until they have provided all of this information.

- **Company** This column will track the name of the client and should therefore be a choice field. When you create the column, choose the type radio button Choice (Menu to Choose From) in the Create Column dialog. After selecting the type, scroll down to the Additional Column Settings section and enter a list of choices in the text box labeled Type Each Choice on a Separate Line. You might also prefer to use the Lookup (Information Already on This Site) data type and query against a list of companies in a separately created Contact List.
- **Date** This column will use the type Date and Time. To make the column more user-friendly, you can set the default value to be today's date.
- **Odometer Start** This will be a number field with a minimum value of 0.
- **Odometer End** This column will be a number field with a minimum value of 1.

- **Total Mileage**   The final column is used to calculate the total mileage. Not surprisingly, this will be a calculated column called Total Mileage. Create the new column using the type Calculated (Calculation Based on Other Columns). Since this field will track the difference between the two odometer readings, the formula to enter is =[Odometer End]-[Odometer Start]. You can create this formula quite easily by typing the equal sign into the Formula text box, double-clicking the first column in the Insert Column list, adding the minus sign, and then double-clicking the second column (see Figure 9-6).

There is a wide range of functionality that can be enabled using calculated fields. For more information about calculated field formulas, refer to the SharePoint documentation online (for example: http://office.microsoft.com/en-us/sharepointtechnology/HA011609471033.aspx).

Once you have created your list, you can start to use it by entering a trip (see Figure 9-7). You'll see that the required fields—in this case, all of them—will appear with a red asterisk. This gives the end user a quick visual clue that they must fill in the field before they can save the new item.

When you add trips to this list, the Total Mileage column will automatically be calculated for you (see Figure 9-8). This can both save time and reduce errors in your reporting.

Hopefully, this real-world example will spark your imagination and you'll come up with some custom lists of your own. Next, we'll take a look at customizing list views.

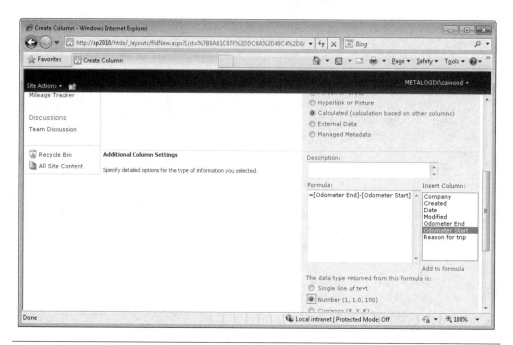

FIGURE 9-6   Adding a calculated field formula

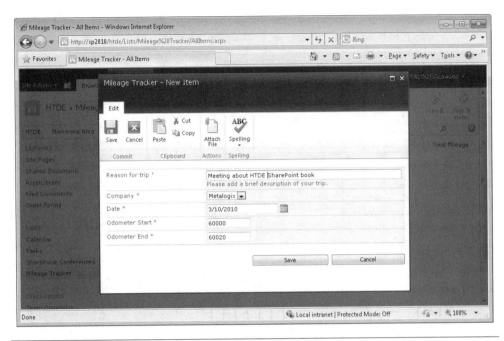

FIGURE 9-7   Adding a trip to the Mileage Tracker custom list

Custom Views

Customized content is one aspect of list customization that you'll likely want to explore further, but that's not the only list adaptation that you'll want to try. Another useful dimension of list augmentation is creating custom views. When you create a list, SharePoint also creates a view that presents the data to you. For example,

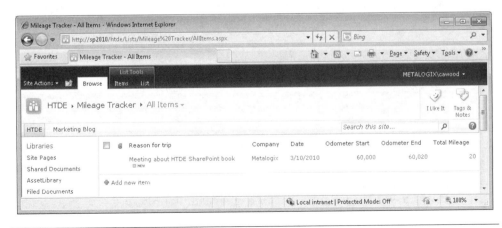

FIGURE 9-8   The Mileage Tracker custom list

a Calendar list actually looks like a calendar, and a document library shows you a simple grid-based overview of your documents.

The view that is used to show a new list is called the default view. Some lists come with more than one view out of the box, so changing to one of the other views is your first option. However, you can also create your own personalized view if you feel that there is a better way to present the data. For example, document libraries only come with one view, All Documents, so if you aren't happy with the default, you'll need to make one to order.

To begin this exercise, select Document Library in the Create dialog and then upload some files. You'll see that the default view shows the columns Type, Name, Modified, and Modified By (see Figure 9-9).

As you saw in the previous exercise, adding a new column to the default view is an option when you create the column. However, there are plenty of columns that aren't shown in the default view. Suppose you want to add a Checked Out To column to the view so that you can see at a glance who has each document checked out. If you want to see this column, you can either create your own view or modify the current view. In this example, click the Modify View button in the Library section of the ribbon.

The Edit View dialog (see Figure 9-10) includes options for changing the name or the view and even changing the URL. The Columns section includes options to add columns and change the sort order.

Simply check the box next to the Checked Out To column and then click OK to save your changes. After you click OK, the default list view will show the Checked Out To column (see Figure 9-11).

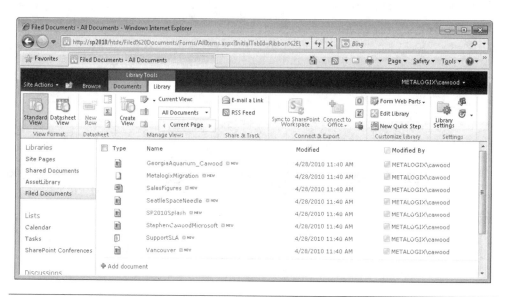

FIGURE 9-9 The default view for a document library

Name

Type a name for this view of the document library. Make the name descriptive, such as "Sorted by Author", so that site visitors will know what to expect when they click this link.

View Name:

All Documents

Web address of this view:

http://sp2010/htde/Filed Documents/Forms/ AllItems

.aspx

This view appears by default when visitors follow a link to this document library. If you want to delete this view, first make another view the default.

⊟ Columns

Select or clear the check box next to each column you want to show or hide in this view of this page. To specify the order of the columns, select a number in the **Position from left** box.

Display	Column Name	Position from Left
☑	Type (icon linked to document)	1 ▾
☑	Name (linked to document with edit menu)	2 ▾
☑	Modified	3 ▾
☑	Modified By	4 ▾
☐	Check In Comment	5 ▾
☑	Checked Out To	6 ▾

FIGURE 9-10   Customizing the default view

If modifying an existing view isn't going to work for you, you can also choose to create a new view. For example, suppose that most of your users want to use the default view but a few want to have an additional view. If this is the case, you can use the Create View button on the ribbon to create a brand new view. When you choose this option, you're asked to pick from the available built-in views:

- **Standard View**   View data on a web page. You can choose from a list of display styles. Use this view type to show each instance of a recurring event.
- **Datasheet View**   View data in an editable spreadsheet format that is convenient for bulk editing and quick customization. To use this view, you'll need the Office

☐ Type	Name	Modified	☐ Modified By	☐ Checked Out To
	GeorgiaAquarium_Cawood	4/28/2010 11:40 AM	METALOGIX\cawood	METALOGIX\cawood
☐	MetalogixMigration	4/28/2010 11:40 AM	METALOGIX\cawood	
	SalesFigures	4/28/2010 11:40 AM	METALOGIX\cawood	
	SeatlleSpaceNeedle	4/28/2010 11:40 AM	METALOGIX\cawood	METALOGIX\cawood
	SP2010Splash	4/28/2010 11:40 AM	METALOGIX\cawood	
	StephenCawoodMicrosoft	4/28/2010 11:40 AM	METALOGIX\cawood	
	SupportSLA	4/28/2010 11:40 AM	METALOGIX\cawood	
	Vancouver	4/28/2010 11:40 AM	METALOGIX\cawood	

➕ Add document

FIGURE 9-11   After modifying the default list view

SharePoint components installed. These are available if you have installed Microsoft Office on your local computer.

- **Calendar View**   View data as a daily, weekly, or monthly calendar.
- **Gantt View**   View list items in a Gantt chart to see a graphical representation of how a team's tasks relate over time.
- **Access View**   Start Microsoft Office Access to create forms and reports that are based on this list. This view also requires the Office SharePoint components.
- **Custom View in SharePoint Designer**   Start SharePoint Designer to create a new view for this list with capabilities such as conditional formatting.

If none of the previous options suits your needs, then it is time to dive into the last one on the list, Custom View in SharePoint Designer.

Custom Views in SharePoint Designer

Microsoft SharePoint Designer 2010 is a free application that you can use to further customize SharePoint. For example, you can also add columns and create views by using SharePoint Designer. However, it's important to note that SharePoint Designer can do much more. To give you an introduction to SharePoint Designer, this first example covers much of the same ground already covered in this chapter. If you're interested in SharePoint Designer, you can download it for free from the Microsoft website.

The first thing to do, obviously, is to start SharePoint Designer. Once it's open, you can connect to any SharePoint site assuming, of course, that you have sufficient permissions to the site. To create a connection, simply click the Open Site button and then provide the URL to the site (see Figure 9-12).

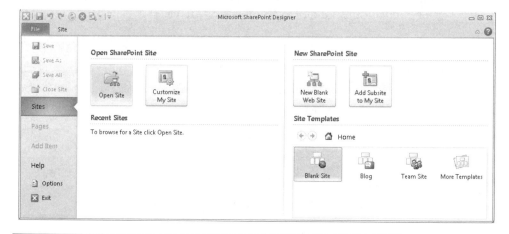

FIGURE 9-12   The Open Site button in SharePoint Designer 2010

You don't need to connect to the root site on the server; you can supply the URL of any subsite if that is where you need to work. Once the site is open, you'll see the content of the site, some general information, and the permissions that have been applied to the site (see Figure 9-13).

At this point, you'll notice that there are quite a few options available to you. However, the goal of this exercise is to create a custom view, so click the Lists and Libraries button in the Site Objects list on the left side. Once you click the button, you'll be shown all of the existing lists and libraries under the selected site. To open one for editing, simply click on it. In the example shown in Figure 9-14, the Filed Documents library was selected.

On the right side, you'll see a list of the views under the selected library. Click the New button above the list and you'll be asked to supply the name of the new custom view (see Figure 9-15). The new view in this example will show all of the approval status columns, so the name selected is Content Approval.

When you click OK, your new view will be added to the list. To edit the view, right-click it and choose Edit File in Advanced Mode. Once you have the view open, you can change it in any way you would like (see Figure 9-16).

At this point, you could switch the view to Code view (or Split view) and edit the HTML for the view. However, the goal of this exercise is to show some columns, so editing the code underlying the page is not necessary. Click the data grid that contains the columns and then click Add/Remove Columns in the Options tab of the ribbon. This opens the Displayed Fields dialog, which enables you to select what should be displayed in the view. In this example, all of the fields related to content approval were selected (see Figure 9-17).

FIGURE 9-13   A site open in SharePoint Designer 2010

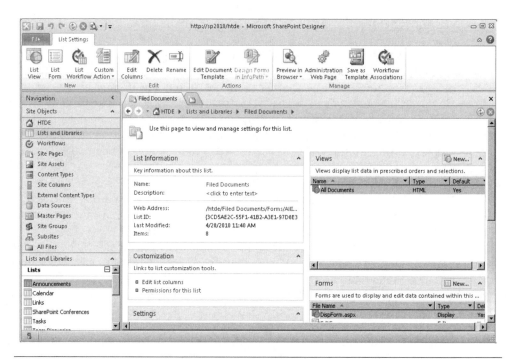

FIGURE 9-14 A document library open for editing

Once you save your changes, you can go back to the document library in the browser and select the new view. You can now quickly see data such as who has a document checked out or what was written in the latest checked-in comment (see Figure 9-18).

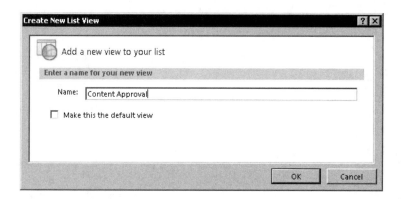

FIGURE 9-15 Creating a new custom view

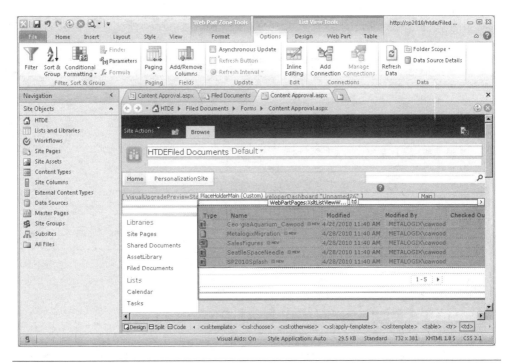

FIGURE 9-16   A list view open in Advanced Mode

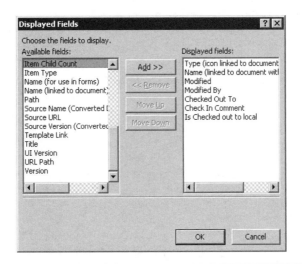

FIGURE 9-17   Choosing which fields to display

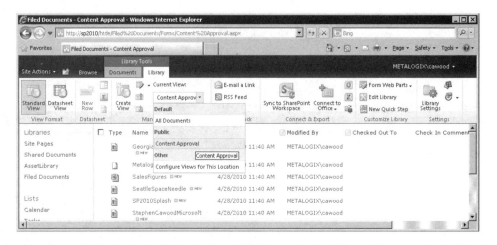

FIGURE 9-18 Selecting the new custom list view

Per-Location View Settings

Now that you've created a custom view, you may be wondering if that view has to be available everywhere. The answer is no, you can use per-location view settings to define where each view will be available. For example, you may want to use one view for the root of a document library, but a different view for everything inside folders.

To open the settings, find the Current View section under the Library tab of the ribbon and expand the drop-down menu for the available views. At the bottom, choose Configure Views for This Location. Alternatively, you can open the List Settings from the Library tab on the ribbon and then choose the link for Per-Location View Settings. In this example, the option to break inheritance is chosen on a folder in the document library and the new Content Approval view is hidden (see Figure 9-19). This means that the view will be available at the root of the library, but not in the folder.

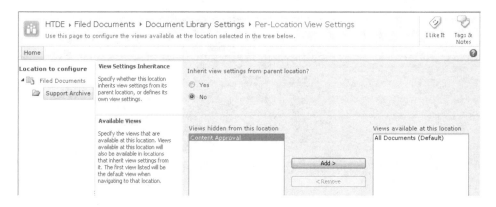

FIGURE 9-19 Choosing which views are available

Site Customizations

Hopefully, the previous section has sparked your interest in the customization potential of lists. Now it's time to move up to the site level. Just like lists, there are many options when it comes to site customization. This section explores those possibilities.

Themes

The site theme determines the general appearance of a SharePoint site. For example, it defines the color scheme. In this way, it's similar to a Windows theme, or the Appearance setting in Microsoft Outlook Web Access.

To alter a SharePoint site theme, choose Site Actions | Site Settings and then choose Site Theme from the Look and Feel section of the Site Settings page. When the Site Theme page opens, you can customize the site colors and fonts and even preview your customization before applying the change (see Figure 9-20).

 Create your SharePoint themes in Microsoft PowerPoint. If you want, you can even design a theme in Microsoft PowerPoint, save it as a new Office Theme File type (.thmx extension), and then upload it to the Themes gallery and apply it to your site.

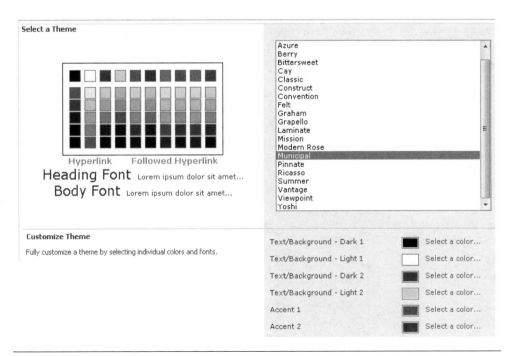

FIGURE 9-20   Site theme options

Customizing Navigation

When planning a website, navigation planning can be downright daunting. After all, what defines the usability of a website more than its navigation? The Microsoft Office teams spend considerable time thinking about navigation. I know this because, during my time as a Program Manager at Microsoft, I helped design the navigation for Microsoft Office SharePoint Server 2007. Of course, more than just thinking is involved; the Office team also makes use of usability studies to help figure out the best possible navigation for SharePoint.

An essential part of providing user-friendly navigation is allowing SharePoint customers the opportunity to customize various navigation elements to suit their business requirements. If you would like to make changes to your navigation, there are two angles from which to approach the changes:

- Go to the object in question (for example, a list of a site) and choose to show or hide it in the navigation
- Go to the navigation settings of the parent site and choose how the navigation will behave at the site level

The second option is clearly more powerful because you can make decisions that apply to many lists, libraries, pages, or subsites below the parent site. To make changes at the site level, choose Site Actions | Site Settings and then find the Look and Feel section. The navigation settings include the following:

 Quick Launch and Top Link Bar won't appear in the settings if publishing is turned on. Instead, there will be an option for Navigation.

- **Quick launch** The quick launch appears down the left side of the page and is used on most SharePoint pages. When you choose to edit the quick launch settings, you can add or remove items and change the sort order (see Figure 9-21). If you don't like the heading, you can add your own by clicking New Heading.

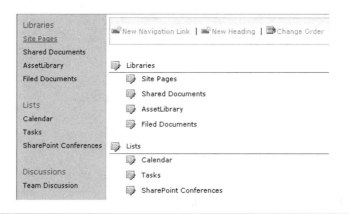

FIGURE 9-21 Editing the quick launch navigation

FIGURE 9-22   The tree view navigation

 If something does not appear in the quick launch (for example, a page or a list), check the settings of that object. It may have been hidden from the quick launch.

- **Top link bar**   As you'd expect, the top link bar appears at the top of the page. When you open the settings for the top link bar, you have options to edit the existing links, add a new one, and change the display order. The last option is Use Links from Parent. If you select this option, the current links will be deleted and the top link bar links from the parent site will replace them. Some users prefer to have the top link bar the same on every page and subsite; this option can be used to implement that type of navigation and consistency.
- **Tree view**   The tree view is usually disabled, but if you'd like to have a handy hierarchical view of the site content, then click the Tree View link in Site Settings and choose to enable this option. The only option for this control is to turn it on or off. When it is enabled, you can click the arrow image to expand the hierarchy—just like you would in Windows Explorer (see Figure 9-22).

Custom Forms

Microsoft InfoPath electronic forms can be huge time savers. Instead of producing paper forms that might eventually end up being scanned for archiving anyway, why not just cut out the middle steps and go directly to digital?

In this example scenario, you're going to add a new electronic form to SharePoint that will collect the information for a product order. Once you are finished, you'll be able to navigate to the form library in SharePoint, add a new item, and be presented with the custom form to fill out. Each time you fill one out, it will be saved in the form library.

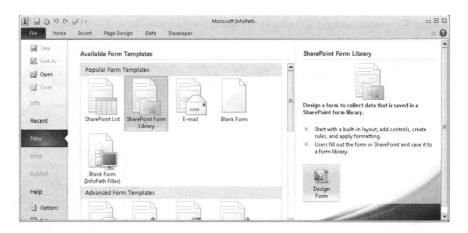

FIGURE 9-23 Selecting the SharePoint form template in InfoPath 2010

 This example will only work completely in SharePoint Server 2010 Enterprise Edition because InfoPath Forms Services is not available in other versions. For example, SharePoint Foundation does not offer this functionality.

To start the process, you need to create the form template in Microsoft InfoPath Designer 2010. If you have InfoPath installed, you can try this example. First, open InfoPath Designer from the Start menu, select the SharePoint Form Library template, and then click Design Form (see Figure 9-23).

After you make your choice, InfoPath will open the template for editing. In this case, you're creating an order form, so change the title to Order Form and change the first heading to Personal Information. To make these changes, simply click on the text and start typing. This example is meant to be straightforward, so only the Name field has been added (see Figure 9-24).

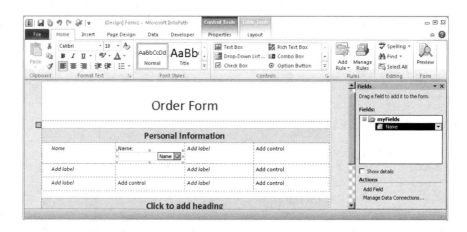

FIGURE 9-24 The new form in edit mode

To allow users to enter information into the form, you'll need to add fields. To add the Name field, click in the Add Control cell next to Add Label and type **Name**. On the right side of the page, expand the drop-down list under myFields and choose Add. When you do so, the Add Field or Group Properties dialog opens and you can enter the name and data type for your field (see Figure 9-25). In this case, you can call the field Name and use the data type Text (String). Click OK.

At this point you may want to save your form locally so that you have a backup copy. To do this, just click the Save button on the ribbon and choose a folder. Next, you'll be publishing the form template to a SharePoint form library. Fortunately, InfoPath makes this whole process pain free. You can do everything from within the client.

To publish your new custom form template, switch to the InfoPath File menu and then select the Publish tab on the left side of the application (see Figure 9-26).

The first thing you'll be asked is which SharePoint site you'd like to use to host the form template. Enter the URL of the site that will contain the form. For example, the URL of the example site used in this sample is http://sp2010/htde.

After you enter the URL, the Publishing Wizard will start and give you a few choices: Do you want the form to be used from a browser? What would you like to create or modify? For the first choice, you should check the box to enable the option. For the second, you'll want to choose Form Library (see Figure 9-27).

This rest of this example will only work with SharePoint Server 2010 Enterprise Edition. You can, however, continue with the example by clearing the Enable This Form to Be Filled Out by Using a Browser check box. This means that using your form will require the InfoPath client instead.

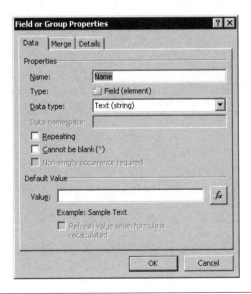

FIGURE 9-25   Adding a new field to the form

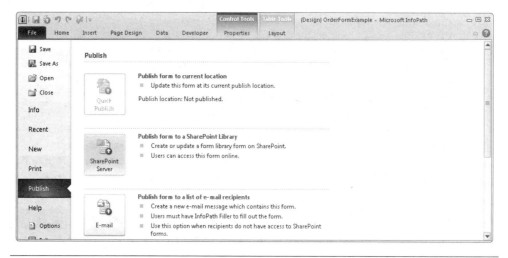

FIGURE 9-26 The Publishing tab in InfoPath 2010

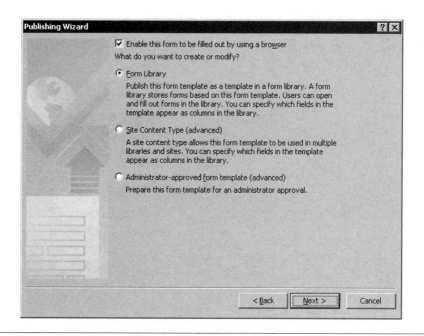

FIGURE 9-27 Choosing the first of the form publishing options

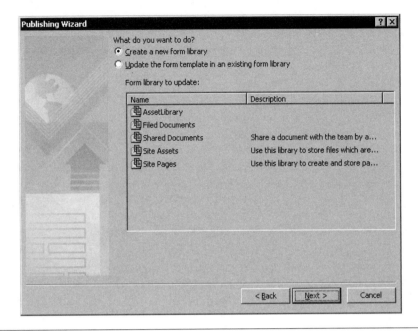

FIGURE 9-28   Choosing where to upload the form

After selecting the options in the first dialog, click Next to continue to the next one. The next step allows you to either create a new form library in SharePoint or upload your custom form template to an existing library (see Figure 9-28). Creating the form library from the publishing step is a handy option because InfoPath manages the whole process for you instead of requiring you to complete the manual steps of creating a library and assigning the InfoPath template. Therefore, use the first option in this example. Click Next and you'll be asked to supply a name for your new library.

After adding the name, and possibly a description as well, click Next again. At this point, you'll decide which form fields will be available as columns within SharePoint. In this example, you want your Name field to be added because that will allow users to sort and filter the orders by the name. Click the Add button in the column section of the dialog. This opens the Select a Field or Group dialog and allows you to choose the Name field from your custom form (see Figure 9-29). Once you click OK, it will appear in the column section of the available fields.

When you click Next, you will be presented with a summary of some of your choices and you can either go back or click the Publish button to proceed. After publishing your form template, you will receive a success message. Choose the Open this Form Library option so that you can try out your new form template (see Figure 9-30).

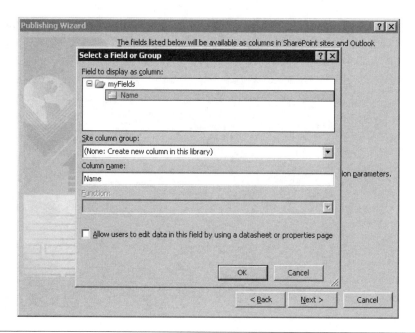

FIGURE 9-29 Adding the Name field as a column in SharePoint

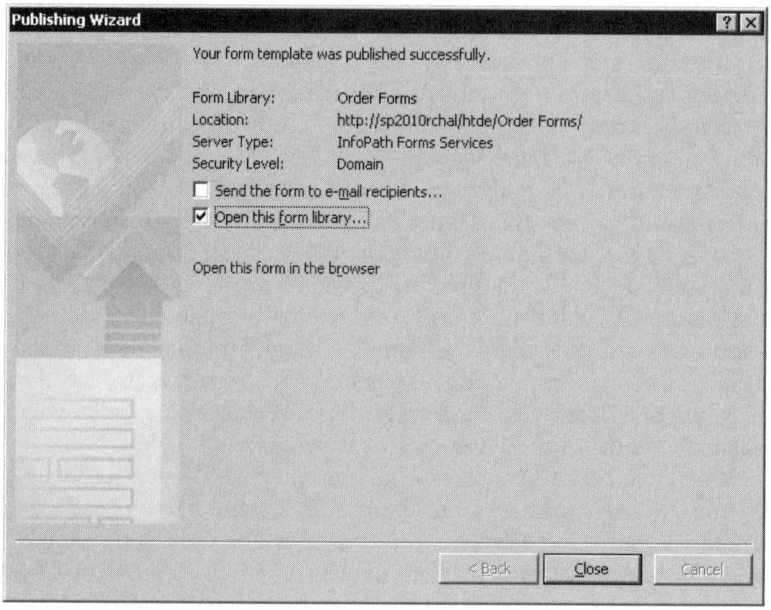

FIGURE 9-30 After publishing the form template to SharePoint

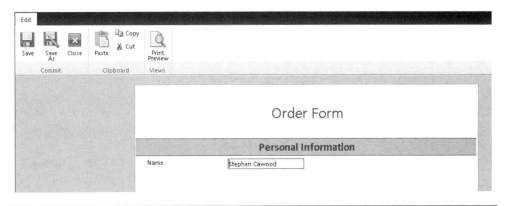

FIGURE 9-31 Adding an order using the new form template

When you choose to continue, InfoPath will open the new form library for you. Of course, it will be empty, so you'll want to choose Add Document to create an order. Since you chose to allow web editing, this will open the form directly in Internet Explorer and allow you to enter the name into the Name field (see Figure 9-31).

Once you have entered the name, click the Save button and then close the order. SharePoint will return you to the form library, where you can see that the order has been created and the name you entered is visible in the Name column of the documents list (see Figure 9-32). Congratulations, you've created your own customized SharePoint form using InfoPath!

The customization options within SharePoint are numerous and varied. This chapter is meant to give you a taste of that variety. If you're interested in learning more about specific aspects of customizing SharePoint, search online for videos or blog tutorials related to your topic of interest. Just bear in mind that SharePoint customization and development is a massive topic, so it's best to have specific objectives in mind and start with small projects. Have fun!

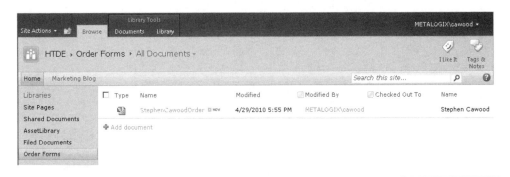

FIGURE 9-32 After adding an order to the library

10

Using SharePoint with Client Applications

HOW TO...

- Use Microsoft Office Backstage
- Use the Connect to Office option
- Work with SharePoint through Microsoft Outlook
- Take SharePoint offline using SharePoint Workspace
- Create forms with Microsoft InfoPath
- Customize SharePoint with SharePoint Designer
- Use third-party clients with SharePoint

The goal of this chapter is to introduce you to some of the rich clients that you can use with SharePoint. There are many reasons why people choose to use these applications. For example, some software makes certain tasks easier, and some client programs enable use cases that simply aren't available through the SharePoint web-based user interface.

Microsoft Office Backstage

The new Microsoft Office 2010 Backstage view replaces the traditional File menu that you would have seen in previous versions of Office. To try it out, open Microsoft Word 2010 and create a new document. Once you have your document ready to save into SharePoint, click the File tab to open the Backstage view and then choose Save & Send | Save to SharePoint (see Figure 10-1).

If you've already saved a document to SharePoint, you will be shown the last location in the Recent Locations area. However, if it is the first time you've used this feature, you need to use the Save As button. When you click Save As, you'll be asked

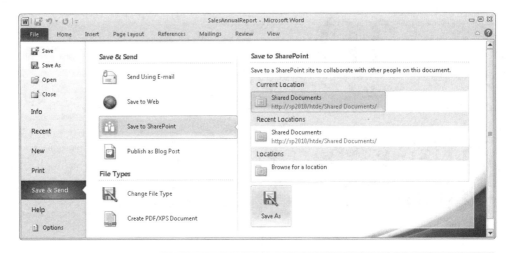

FIGURE 10-1 The new Office Backstage view open in Microsoft Word

where you'd like to save the document (see Figure 10-2). You can enter the URL of your SharePoint server in the address box at the top of the dialog. To do this, click the little folder icon and then paste in the URL address of your SharePoint site. The dialog will show the available SharePoint document libraries and you'll be able to choose where you want to save the file.

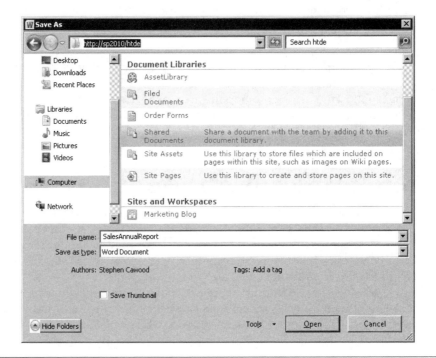

FIGURE 10-2 Saving to a SharePoint document library

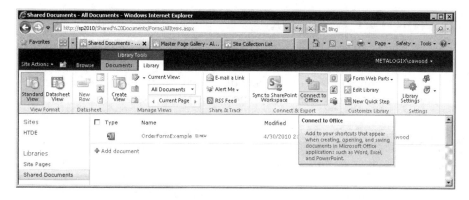

FIGURE 10-3   The Connect to Office button in the ribbon

Connect to Office

If you want to continue to use Office applications to save files in SharePoint, you can quickly add lists to the Favorites section of the Backstage browse dialog. To do this, you can use the Connect to Office button in the SharePoint ribbon (see Figure 10-3). To add the current list to the Favorites list in the Backstage dialog, simply open a list and then click the button.

After you have selected to connect the document library to Office, it appears in the list of SharePoint sites in the Save As dialog (see Figure 10-4).

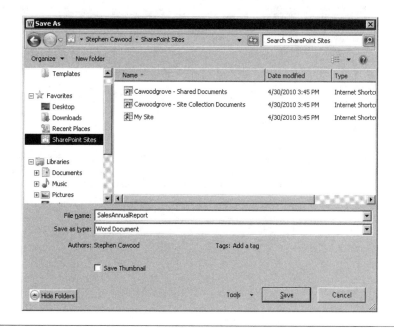

FIGURE 10-4   The list of connected SharePoint libraries

Microsoft Outlook

From an end-user perspective, Microsoft Outlook is probably the most integrated of the SharePoint client applications. From Outlook, you can connect to many types of lists, including contacts, tasks, and discussion boards, view and edit calendars, or even upload files to SharePoint by sending attachments to e-mail–enabled lists.

 Tip Subscribe to a SharePoint RSS feed from within Outlook to get content delivered straight to your Inbox. For example, you can subscribe to a SharePoint blog and not have to worry about going to the blog page to check for updates.

In this example, you'll connect a discussion board list to Outlook so that you can read and contribute from within Outlook. To set it up, first navigate to the list and then click the Connect to Outlook button on the ribbon (see Figure 10-5).

After you confirm that you'd like to connect the list to Outlook, SharePoint will open Outlook for you (see Figure 10-6).

Many people find that they spend most of their time in their e-mail client. If you're one of them, you may appreciate the ability to reply directly to a SharePoint discussion thread from within the application that you already have open (see Figure 10-7).

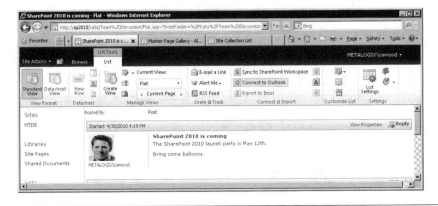

FIGURE 10-5 Connecting to a discussion board list in SharePoint

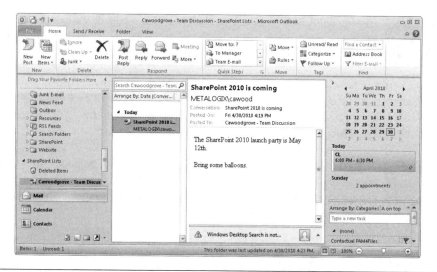

FIGURE 10-6   The discussion list open in Outlook

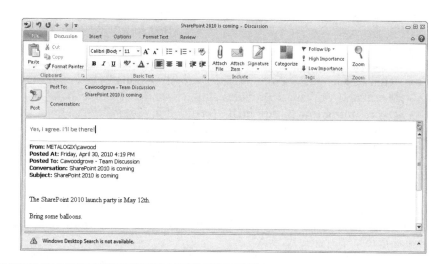

FIGURE 10-7   Replying to a SharePoint thread from Outlook

You can right-click on any SharePoint list from within Outlook and choose Open in Web Browser. Also, you can "share" the list with others by right-clicking and sending colleagues direct links via e-mail to wire their Outlook client to the list.

If you would like to see your SharePoint calendar from within Outlook, you can view or edit it by connecting a calendar list to the client. Back in SharePoint 2003, calendars were read-only in Outlook, but in recent versions, you can make changes to calendars. This is very useful, particularly if you use the Outlook overlay mode.

 Calendars are another type of list that can be e-mail enabled. After you have connected the calendar, you can choose to share the calendar with other people by sending them an e-mail. This allows you to quickly create a shared office calendar system.

SharePoint Workspace

SharePoint Workspace, which was formerly known as Microsoft Groove, allows you to take your SharePoint lists and libraries offline—and this includes external lists that might be bringing information from backend systems. According to Arpan Shah's blog (http://blogs.msdn.com/b/arpans/archive/2010/04/09/sharepoint-workspace-2010.aspx), there are three primary values of SharePoint Workspace:

- **Offline capability**   Whether you are traveling on an airplane or just have spotty network access, SharePoint Workspace allows you to take your content offline.
- **Rich experience**   From drag-and-drop functionality to better performance, SharePoint Workspace provides all the benefits of a rich client.
- **Overcoming low bandwidth**   SharePoint Workspace is a great way to replicate content on the desktop. It synchronizes in the background, so you always have the latest version of your content on your desktop. This avoids the challenge of downloading a very large file on demand over a low-bandwidth/high-latency network.

Since it's a rich client, SharePoint workspaces also provides quick and easy navigation among lists and libraries. You can simply click from one to another without waiting for web pages to load.

To use SharePoint Workspace, you'll need to connect to a SharePoint server. First, open the application, choose Create a New Account, and supply your information. Next, choose SharePoint Workspace from the New drop-down menu (see Figure 10-8).

As you can see, Workspace provides functionality other than synchronizing with SharePoint. For example, you can also use it to create a folder that's shared between computers.

FIGURE 10-8   Creating a new SharePoint workspace

After you supply the URL to a SharePoint site, Workspace will begin to synchronize with your chosen site (see Figure 10-9).

 You cannot download all content types with SharePoint Workspace. For example, you cannot download from a calendar, survey, or wiki.

After adding a site to SharePoint Workspace, many features will be available to you through the client (see Figure 10-10). For example, you can drag and drop to upload files to a document library.

FIGURE 10-9 SharePoint Workspace synchronizing with a site

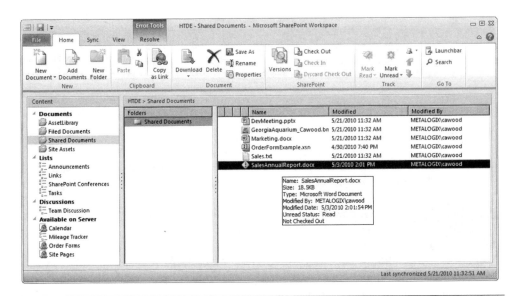

FIGURE 10-10 A site open in SharePoint Workspace

Microsoft InfoPath 2010

Microsoft InfoPath 2010 can be used to create custom electronic forms for use in SharePoint. InfoPath provides many powerful features for building new forms or converting existing forms. You can use the client to create a form template and then use that template in a SharePoint form library. An example of using InfoPath to create a custom form was provided in Chapter 9.

SharePoint Designer

Microsoft SharePoint Designer is a free client application that provides added customization options for SharePoint 2010. If you want to do a lot of SharePoint development, Microsoft Visual Studio 2010 would be the tool of choice, but if you need to create custom master pages, add custom lists, or create powerful new views or custom formatting, then SharePoint Designer is the right choice. You can also use SharePoint Designer to create new lists, add or remove columns, edit the properties of lists, or even create new master pages.

An example of using SharePoint Designer to create a custom list view was provided in Chapter 9.

Colligo Contributor

Of course, not all SharePoint client applications are created by Microsoft. There are dozens of independent software vendors (ISVs) that create software for SharePoint. One such company is Colligo Incorporated—the developers of Colligo Contributor (www.colligo.com).

The award-winning Colligo Contributor client software suite drives SharePoint adoption by enabling users to more easily work with SharePoint content from within popular desktop applications—including Microsoft Outlook and Windows Explorer. Information workers can use Colligo Contributor online or offline to instantly edit, view, or create documents, e-mails, forms, lists, or metadata in SharePoint. The suite includes the following products:

- **Colligo Contributor File Manager**   Seamlessly links folders on users' file systems with SharePoint document libraries. Local folders become "SharePoint aware" so users can access advanced features, such as metadata, content types, and document templates. These folders can be accessed from any application that uses the standard Windows File Open/Save dialog.
- **Colligo Contributor Add-In for Outlook**   Delivers access to SharePoint libraries and lists—all from within Microsoft Office Outlook. Users can easily save e-mails to SharePoint by clicking the Send & File button or simply dragging and dropping e-mails into document libraries and folders. The add-in will automatically capture e-mail properties as metadata. The e-mail attachment manager automatically saves attachments to SharePoint and replaces them with links.

- **Colligo Contributor Client** Enhances productivity and adoption by enabling mobile workers to instantly and securely access, modify, and create SharePoint content anywhere through a rich client interface. Changes made offline to libraries and lists are automatically synchronized to SharePoint when the user goes back online.
- **Colligo Contributor Pro** Offers the ultimate desktop integration for SharePoint. This product includes the previously described user interfaces: the rich stand-alone desktop client, Add-In for Outlook, and even a Windows Explorer extension.

A Colligo for SharePoint folder can be synched with a SharePoint 2010 document library and then opened in Windows Explorer (see Figure 10-11). When this is set up, the column headings in Windows Explorer are actually the column headings from the SharePoint 2010 document library. Also, common Windows Explorer functions such as sorting and grouping can be used to organize the files using metadata values. For example, Name and Products are conventional SharePoint columns, Document ID is a new feature available in SharePoint 2010, and Home Location is a new managed metadata column. All of the content in the document library is available both online and offline as it has been cached on the client.

In the example shown in Figure 10-11, the user has right-clicked on one of the e-mails stored in the document library and selected Edit Properties. This instantly brings up a dialog that is a rich client editor for SharePoint metadata. In this case, the user is picking a metadata term using the taxonomy-service browser. In addition to making

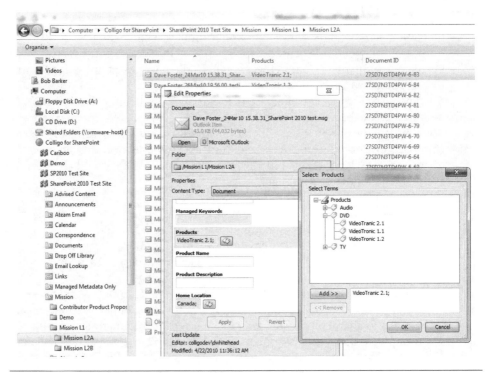

FIGURE 10-11 Using a Colligo for SharePoint folder from Windows Explorer

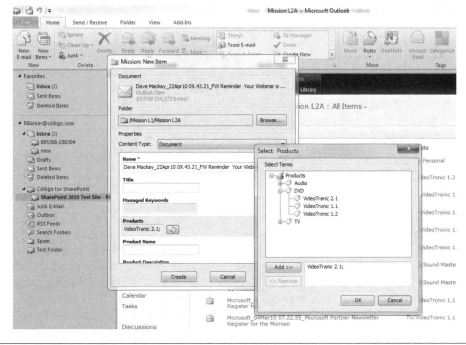

FIGURE 10-12   Dragging an e-mail into SharePoint

SharePoint document libraries available in Windows Explorer and caching content, the Colligo Windows Explorer extension supports Open and Save As operations (with full metadata capture) to SharePoint document libraries from within any desktop application.

The Colligo suite can also be used to synchronize Microsoft Outlook with a SharePoint 2010 document library (see Figure 10-12). The user can choose not to cache the library, so the actual SharePoint site will be displayed (as in the background of Figure 10-12) within the Outlook interface when the user clicks on the SharePoint folder. In this example, the user has dragged-and-dropped an e-mail from her inbox into the SharePoint 2010 Test Site folder so that she can save it in SharePoint. This action automatically extracts all the e-mail properties (over 20 of them) and maps them to SharePoint metadata. Once the user clicks Create, the e-mail, attachments, extracted metadata, and custom metadata are automatically stored in SharePoint.

Metalogix Site Migration Manager

Another prominent SharePoint ISV is Metalogix Software Corporation—it also happens to be where I have my day job (www.metalogix.net). Metalogix offers a number of Microsoft SharePoint and Microsoft Exchange administration solutions, but is best known for SharePoint migration, archiving and storage management. The Metalogix migration applications include SharePoint upgrade and support numerous source systems. Whether you're looking to move content to SharePoint from file shares, other web systems, or earlier versions of SharePoint, Metalogix has a product that will help.

However, the products are not just for migration. Metalogix SharePoint Site Migration Manager (SSMM) offers a number of management features that make it a useful SharePoint client application. For example, Metalogix SSMM 2010 can do the following:

- Move assets such as lists or sites to different servers or different locations
- Split list contents or merge lists together
- Migrate SharePoint sites, lists, and libraries between servers
- Upgrade from SharePoint 2003 and SharePoint 2007 to SharePoint 2010
- Reorganize or re-template your SharePoint content
- Migrate to hosted SharePoint environments such as Microsoft's Business Productivity Online Suite (BPOS)
  Visit www.metalogix.net to download a free trial of SSMM 2010 (see Figure 10-13).

 Note Colligo and Metalogix are not the only third-party vendors creating management software for SharePoint. If you're looking for SharePoint client applications, take some time to surf the Web and check out what's available. Many companies offer free trial downloads so that you can see their applications in action before you buy. You can also read reviews on sites such as SharePoint Reviews, www .sharepointreviews.com.

As you've seen throughout this chapter, there are many SharePoint client options. Whether you're just a fan of rich clients or you need the power of a product such as SharePoint Designer, you may find that you prefer to interact with SharePoint through an interface other than a web browser.

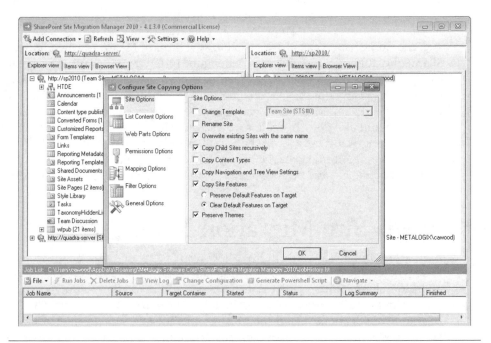

FIGURE 10-13   Metalogix SharePoint Site Migration Manager 2010

11

Template Reference for Libraries, Lists, Pages, and Sites

HOW TO...

- Learn about site templates
- Use various list and library templates
- Differentiate between types of SharePoint pages

As already mentioned in this book, the end-user functionality within SharePoint is largely determined by the list templates, site templates, and web parts that are provided out of the box. This chapter is a reference for the libraries, lists, pages, and sites that are available in SharePoint Server 2010.

Remember that some of the following list or library types may not be available on your server. Your options will depend upon the version of SharePoint you are using, the features that are installed, and the site template for the current site. For example, if you're using SharePoint Server 2010 with the Enterprise features enabled, you will see most, if not all, of the templates listed in this chapter.

Many of the templates that fit into this chapter have already been discussed in other parts of this book; in those cases you can follow the reference to the relevant chapter. Conversely, some of the important templates that didn't fit nicely into the other chapter topics will be covered here. For your convenience, the description of each template is included from the SharePoint UI.

Libraries

Libraries are actually lists—lists with attachments. Whether you need to manage documents, images, or forms, SharePoint can help make the task easier. Libraries combine the benefits of SharePoint lists with features specific to the type of content being stored.

Asset Library

A place to share, browse and manage rich media assets, like image, audio and video files.

If you're looking for a central place to store image, audio, and video files, an asset library might be the right choice for you. One advantage of using an asset library is the various metadata that's made available as part of the list template. For example, you can specify whether the file is an image file, an audio file, or a video (see Figure 11-1). If you were working on a presentation that required various types of media, this library would allow you to store them in one location and then filter by the metadata, such as the media type.

The asset library in SharePoint 2010 features a new video control that allows you to easily share video within SharePoint. Upload a WMV video file and you can play it directly from SharePoint.

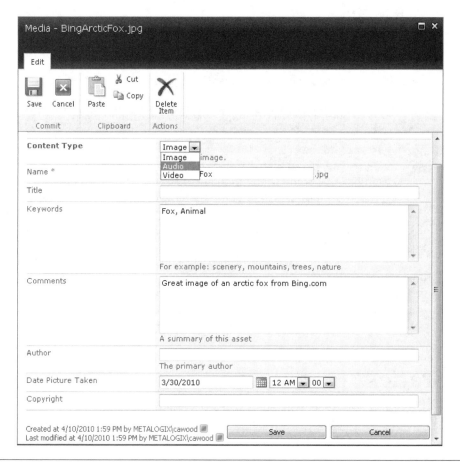

FIGURE 11-1 Asset library item options

Data Connection Library

A place where you can easily share files that contain information about external data connections.

Data connection libraries are used to store files that define data connections. This includes Office Data Connection (ODC) files and Universal Data Connection (UDC) files. These files can define connections to databases, web services, or even SharePoint libraries or lists.

By storing these connection files in SharePoint, you can use InfoPath to leverage these connections and use them when creating InfoPath forms. For example, if I know that my team will be using a web service to gather data that will be used in our InfoPath forms, I can create a data connection file in InfoPath and store that file in a data connection library, thereby making it easier for anyone who wants to use that connection in their InfoPath forms to do so.

Document Library

A place for storing documents or other files that you want to share. Document libraries allow folders, versioning, and check out.

Document libraries are the backbone of document management in SharePoint. They are covered extensively in Chapter 2.

 Document libraries and certain types of lists can be e-mail enabled to allow you to simply e-mail a document to the library or list instead of uploading the files through the SharePoint web UI.

Form Library

A place to manage business forms like status reports or purchase orders. Form libraries require a compatible XML editor, such as Microsoft InfoPath.

Form libraries can be used with Microsoft InfoPath to create custom electronic forms for your organization. Creating forms is covered in Chapter 9.

Picture Library

A place to upload and share pictures.

The description from Microsoft for the Picture Library template doesn't really provide a full explanation of what these libraries can do. Picture libraries allow you to associate metadata with images, view images in a slide show, convert images to web format, add version control, and use metadata-based filtering. You can even add validation settings to allow you to specify parameters, such as height, that determine whether images can be added to the library. As with many types of lists, you can add optional folders for organization.

To start adding pictures to your picture library, expand the Upload drop-down menu and choose either Upload Picture or Upload Multiple Pictures. In this example, we will choose to upload more than one picture (see Figure 11-2).

If you have installed Microsoft Office and the optional Shared Tools for SharePoint, you'll have the benefit of using Microsoft Office Picture Manager to upload pictures to your picture libraries. Once Office Picture Manager opens, you can create picture shortcuts to directories that you'll reuse. This saves you the time of navigating through your folder structure each time you have new content to add. One of the advantages of using Office Picture Manager is that you'll see a thumbnail image of each picture in the directory you select (see Figure 11-3).

When you upload images, you can choose to downgrade them to web quality (that is, the quality used by web browsers). Since most cameras produce images that have much better quality than the Web, this can save you some storage space and also improve page load times. Of course, the quality of the versions of the images stored in the picture library is likely to be lower than that of the originals, but if the images are going to be used only on the Web, then the downside is insubstantial.

After you upload the images, you can select the link to return to the library, where you'll see your images in the picture library (see Figure 11-4). Once the images have been loaded, you can start using features such as the slide show view.

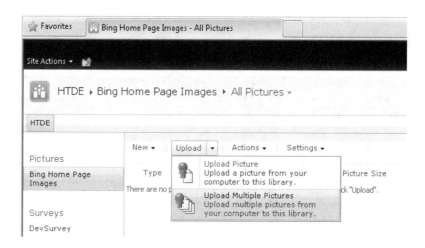

FIGURE 11-2 Choosing to upload multiple images

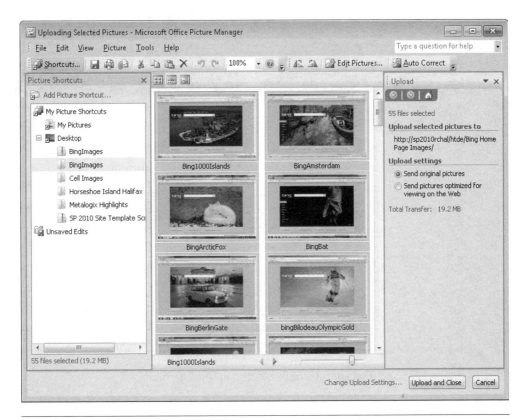

FIGURE 11-3   Selecting the images to upload

As you learned in Chapter 3, you will not get the same upload options in all browsers. For example, if you choose to upload to a picture library using Firefox, you will not be able to use the Upload Multiple Documents control that's available if you use Internet Explorer 8 (see Figure 11-5).

One of the unique features of the picture library is the ability to view the files in a slide show view. To start the show, choose View Slide Show from the Actions menu (see Figure 11-6).

When you start the slide show, a new window will open and allow you to view the images and move back and forth between them (see Figure 11-7).

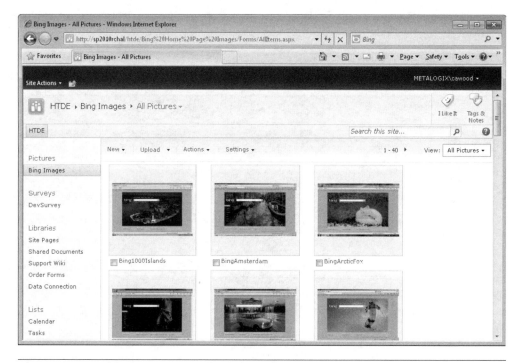

FIGURE 11-4 The picture library after uploading images

FIGURE 11-5 Uploading an image in Firefox

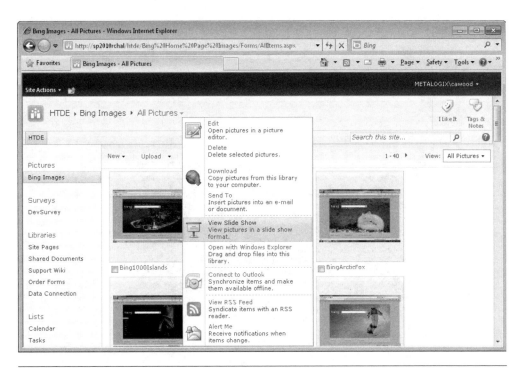

FIGURE 11-6   Selecting the slide show option

Report Library

A place where you can easily create and manage web pages and documents to track metrics, goals and business intelligence information.

Report Libraries provide columns for useful report data such as the owner, status, and report category. All of this data is meant to save you the trouble of adding these columns to a standard document library.

Slide Library

Create a slide library when you want to share slides from Microsoft PowerPoint, or a compatible application. Slide libraries also provide special features for finding, managing, and reusing slides.

Slide libraries will be interesting to you if you need to prepare slides for Microsoft PowerPoint presentations, for example. After you create your slide library, you can choose to upload specific slides from existing presentations (see Figure 11-8).

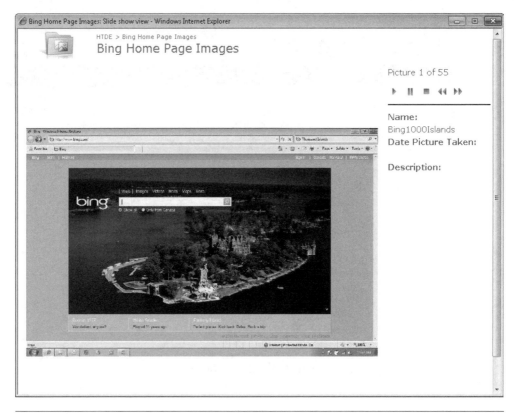

FIGURE 11-7 A picture library slide show

After adding your slides, you'll be able to then easily reuse them in other presentations by choosing the Copy Slide to Presentation option (see Figure 11-9). For example, many presentations have an introduction slide and a slide asking for audience questions. With a slide library, you can upload these reusable elements and then quickly add them to other presentations.

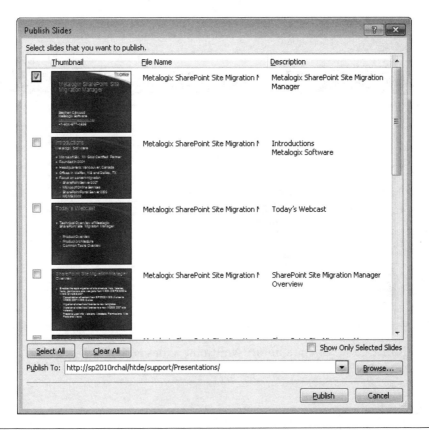

FIGURE 11-8 Choosing PowerPoint slides to add to a slide library

Wiki Page Library

An interconnected set of easily editable web pages, which can contain text, images, and web parts.

Wikis have become mainstream over the last few years. They provide a frictionless, community-authoring environment. Wiki libraries are discussed in Chapter 4.

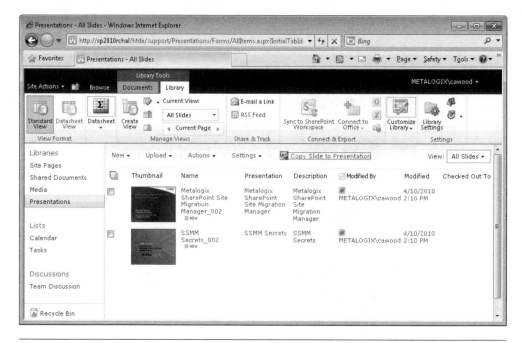

FIGURE 11-9 A slide library with some slides added

Lists

If you polled SharePoint end users, many would identify lists as the fundamental pieces of a SharePoint server. Lists are containers for items—what type of item is determined by the list template.

 At the back end of every SharePoint server is a set of databases, and among those databases, the most heavily used is the content database. List items are rows in that database, and their associated metadata is stored in the columns.

Communications

To make it easier to find what you're looking for, lists are divided into categories in the Create dialog. As the name implies, the Communications category is for lists that help SharePoint users communicate.

Announcements

A list of news items, statuses and other short bits of information.

Announcements help you get out news and updates within your organization. Announcement lists were covered in Chapter 4. Announcements lists are among the handful of list types that can be e-mail enabled. In other words, you can send an e-mail to the announcements list and have it appear in announcement form. The subject line will become the Title, and the body will become the announcement text.

Contacts

A list of people your team works with, like customers or partners. Contacts lists can synchronize with Microsoft Outlook or other compatible programs.

If you need to store a list of contacts in a location that is accessible through a web browser, the SharePoint contacts list can address your needs. When you add a new contact, you'll be asked for all sorts of information such as names, address, e-mail address, and more (see Figure 11-10).

 Contact lists can be linked to Microsoft Outlook and then shared among your team as a global or team contact list.

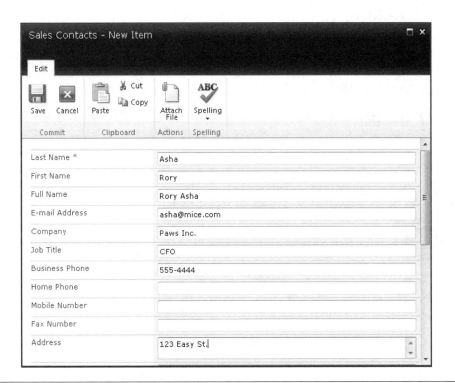

FIGURE 11-10   The new contact dialog

Discussion Board

A place to have newsgroup-style discussions. Discussion boards make it easy to manage discussion threads and can be configured to require approval for all posts.

Discussion boards enable a back-and-forth conversation among people in different locations. This type of list is discussed in Chapter 4.

 Discussion boards can be connected to Microsoft Outlook so that you can carry on a SharePoint conversation using Outlook as your conversation tool.

Links

A list of web pages or other resources.

A links list allows you to store URLs with a description and associated notes. The information that you add to each links list item offers benefits beyond storing the links in a browser's favorites.

Tracking

The Tracking category is probably what people would consider the archetypal usage of lists. You goal is to keep track of a number of items. However, those types of items can obviously be radically different in the business world, and that creates the distinction between the various list templates.

Calendar

A calendar of upcoming meetings, deadlines or other events. Calendar information can be synchronized with Microsoft Outlook or other compatible programs.

Calendar lists provide the functionality that you'd expect from a calendar—and probably a little bit more. Calendars are discussed in Chapter 4.

 Calendars can be connected to Microsoft Outlook so that you can share and overlay SharePoint calendars with your own. As well, calendars are another list type that can be e-mail enabled—you can "invite" a SharePoint calendar to your meetings.

Issue Tracking

A list of issues or problems associated with a project or item. You can assign, prioritize, and track issue status.

An Issue Tracking list is similar to a Tasks list in that you can assign ownership of each item and then track its progress to completion. However, there are a few differences that make tracking issues easier in this type of list. One example is the fact that each issue item is assigned an Issue ID that is visible in the default view of the list. These unique IDs ensure that there is no confusion as to which issues are being discussed.

Status List

A place to track and display a set of goals. Colored icons display the degree to which the goals have been achieved.

Probably the most interesting aspect of a Status List is where the source information is gathered. When you want to track an item, you can use data from a SharePoint list, a Microsoft Excel spreadsheet, or SQL Server Analysis server, or you can manually enter your own data (see Figure 11-11). Once you have added items, they appear with a convenient color-coded symbol that helps you ascertain the current status instantly.

Tasks

A place for team or personal tasks.

Tasks lists are the workhorse of many types of sites in SharePoint. Whether you're creating a meeting workspace or a Team Site, you'll find that you'll automatically get a tasks list.

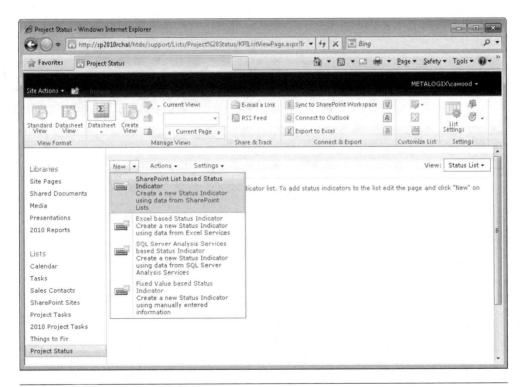

FIGURE 11-11   Status list item options

You don't have to be a proponent of Peter Drucker's management by objectives to understand the importance of tracking granular tasks. SharePoint tasks lists give you the ability to track who owns each task, view what the current priority and status is for each one, and even specify that one or more tasks are predecessors of other tasks (see Figure 11-12).

 Tasks lists, unlike issues lists, can be connected to Microsoft Outlook, so that they can be managed from within the Outlook client.

Project Tasks

A place for team or personal tasks. Project tasks lists provide a Gantt Chart view and can be opened by Microsoft Project or other compatible programs.

The main differences between a regular tasks list and the Projects Tasks list are the default view of your tasks (a Gantt chart in a Projects Tasks list) and the ability to work with the Projects Tasks in Microsoft Project (see Figure 11-13). Also, Project Tasks lists can be linked to Microsoft Outlook.

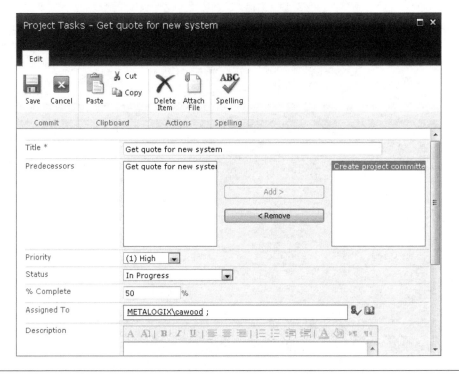

FIGURE 11-12   Creating a new task

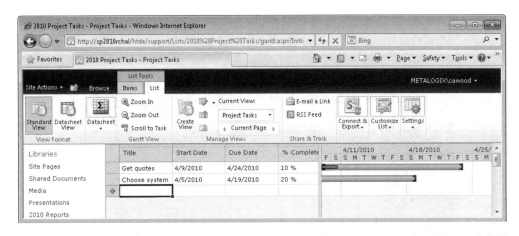

FIGURE 11-13 A project tasks list

Custom Lists

With so many different sites, pages, and lists, people may be led to believe that SharePoint is an application that comes with the functionality they want right out of the box. However, as any large enterprise is already aware, it's simply not possible to develop a one-size-fits-all information management system. Microsoft is keenly aware of this fact and thus has developed SharePoint as a platform; if there is something you need, you can add it. This is where custom lists fit into the picture. If you need to build your own list from scratch, you can still use the functionality that comes with a list, but you can define your own custom type.

Custom List

A blank list to which you can add your own columns and views. Use this if none of the built-in list types are similar to the list you want to make.

The Custom List allows you to start creating your own list with the standard item view as the default. When you create a new custom list, there is only one visible column: Title (see Figure 11-14). It is up to you to build out the rest of the functionality you need.

Custom List in Datasheet View

A blank list which is displayed as a spreadsheet in order to allow easy data entry. You can add your own columns and views. This list type requires a compatible list datasheet ActiveX control, such as the one provided in Microsoft Office.

This type of list also allows you to start with just a Title column, but the default view is a datasheet (see Figure 11-15). As the description states, the datasheet view requires additional software, but it does have its benefits. The datasheet view allows users to quickly make edits to the list data—simply click in a field and start editing.

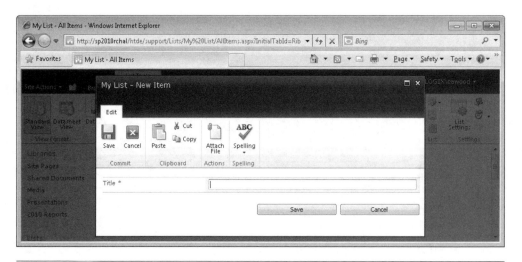

FIGURE 11-14 The Custom List add new item dialog

Import Spreadsheet

Create a list which duplicates the columns and data of an existing spreadsheet. Importing a spreadsheet requires Microsoft Excel or another compatible program.

If you have Microsoft Excel, you'll have the option of importing data quickly from one of your spreadsheets. The Import spreadsheet list allows you to import data from a spreadsheet as part of the list creation process. When you choose to create the list, you'll be asked to specify which spreadsheet file contains the data you would like to import.

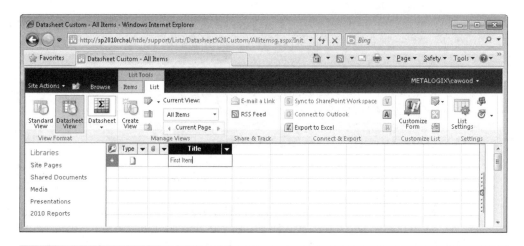

FIGURE 11-15 The Custom List in datasheet view

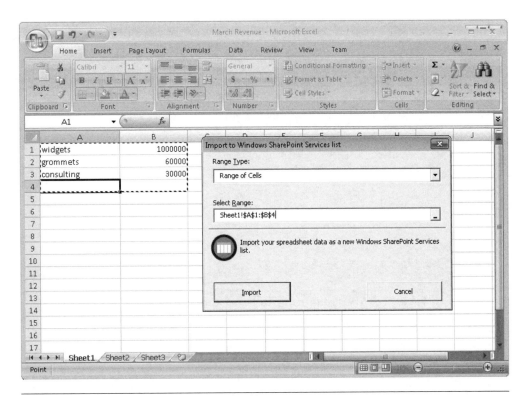

FIGURE 11-16 Choosing a range of cells to import

Then, when you click the Import button, the file will open in Excel and you can choose which cells to import (see Figure 11-16).

After you import the spreadsheet, your data will be imported into the list (see Figure 11-17). Once the import has been completed, there is no connection between the original spreadsheet file and the Import Spreadsheet list.

Data

These lists provide a way to show data collected from various sources.

External List

Create an external list to view the data in an External Content Type.

This list will show data from an external content type, but you will need to first have an external type created by a SharePoint administrator. These lists are used by SharePoint's Business Connectivity Services (BCS). You can define a connection in BCS (often in SharePoint Designer) to an external Microsoft SQL Server database, a Microsoft Access database, or some other type of data source. SharePoint will then present the data as though it were a list in SharePoint.

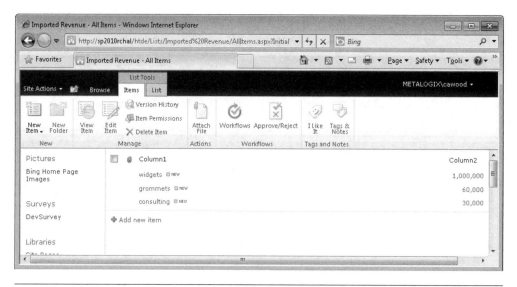

FIGURE 11-17   After importing an Excel spreadsheet

Survey

A list of questions which you would like to have people answer. Surveys allow you to quickly create questions and view graphical summaries of the responses.

Surveys allow you to poll other SharePoint users for their answers to questions you create. Survey lists are discussed in Chapter 4.

Pages

There will be times when you don't need a whole site and a list isn't the right choice. At times, what you want is what some people refer to as a "landing page." Pages allow you to post content in a freeform manner.

Page

A page which can be easily edited in the web browser using Web Edit. Pages can contain text, images, and wiki links, as well as lists and other web parts. Pages are useful for collaborating on small projects.

Obviously, formatted text is available when you create your page content, but you'll also be able to import media such as images, tables, audio, or video. You can even import web parts or SharePoint lists. Pages are created in the Site Pages library, which also supports the use of the wiki page format.

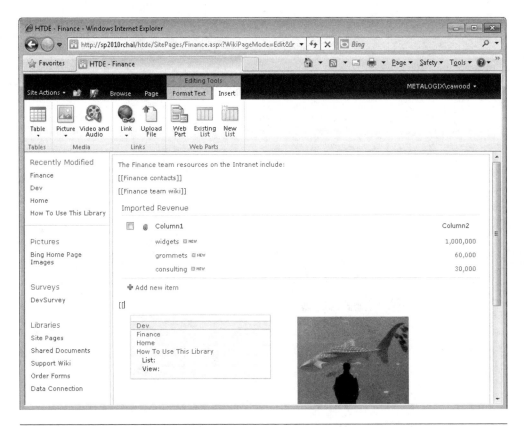

FIGURE 11-18   A page in edit mode

In Figure 11-18, you can see that an image has been imported, but the Import Spreadsheet list from Figure 11-17 has also been added to the page.

 Remember that the wiki functionality of adding page links will also work on pages (see Figure 11-18).

Web Part Page

A page which can display an aggregation of information from other sources. Web part pages can display many types of data, including lists, other web pages, search results, or data retrieved from other servers.

The first versions of SharePoint were called SharePoint Portal Server. The term "portal" is no longer in vogue, but the utility remains. Web part pages embody the idea that SharePoint can be used as a portal into diverse sources of information.

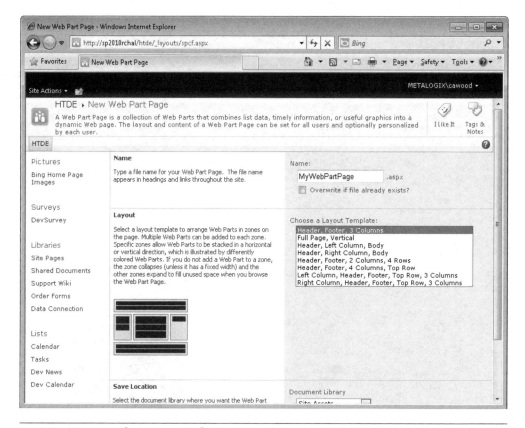

FIGURE 11-19   Choosing a Web Part page layout

Web part pages contain zones, which can contain web parts. When you choose to create a web part page, you'll be asked to choose from a number of different layouts. Each layout contains a different organization option for your page (see Figure 11-19). Or as the Create page dialog explains:

> Select a layout template to arrange Web Parts in zones on the page. Multiple Web Parts can be added to each zone. Specific zones allow Web Parts to be stacked in a horizontal or vertical direction, which is illustrated by differently colored Web Parts. If you do not add a Web Part to a zone, the zone collapses (unless it has a fixed width) and the other zones expand to fill unused space when you browse the Web Part Page.

Numerous web parts come with SharePoint Portal Server 2010. They are discussed in Chapter 8.

Sites

When it comes to information architecture, sites are arguably the most important container in SharePoint planning. Site templates determine the features, lists, and pages that can be created in each area of your SharePoint server. In fact, when people talk about the problem of "SharePoint sprawl," they are generally referring to the creation of too many sites. If your sites are well planned, your users may not feel the need to keep creating more and more.

Blank and Custom

These are the most basic sites available. They give you the freedom to build out what you need.

Blank Site

A blank site for you to customize based on your requirements.

The blank site is the site version of the custom list. Instead of giving you a bunch of pre-created elements, you can add what you need.

Personalization Site

A site for delivering personalized views, data, and navigation from this site collection into My Site. It includes personalization specific Web Parts and navigation that is optimized for My Site sites.

The default content of the Personalization Site template explains how you can use this template to your benefit:

Personalization sites are designed to help you provide an uncompromised distinct personalization experience that connects your portal to users' My Sites. Use this site to push personalized and targeted information to your users based on who they are and why they visit your portal....

After your personalization site is developed, to make your personalization site a permanent location on your users' My Site navigation bar, contact your administrator to register your personalization site.

Personalization sites are discussed in Chapter 7.

Collaboration

The Collaboration category contains site templates that are designed to enable teamwork.

Document Workspace

A site for colleagues to work together on a document. It provides a document library for storing the primary document and supporting files, a tasks list for assigning to-do items, and a links list for resources related to the document.

If collaborating on documents is your primary goal, then a document workspace site is probably right for your needs. Document workspaces are discussed in Chapter 4.

Enterprise Wiki

A site for publishing knowledge that you capture and want to share across the enterprise. It provides an easy content editing experience in a single location for co-authoring content, discussions, and project management.

When you create an Enterprise Wiki site, the default home page content tells you everything you need to know about the site template:

Use the Enterprise Wiki to create a single, go-to place for knowledge sharing and project management across the enterprise. Enterprise Wikis are simple to use, flexible, and lightweight in features. They are quick and easy to create, and you can easily add links to other information systems, corporate directories, or applications....

Working with content—text, graphics, or video—is as easy as working in any word processing application, such as Microsoft Word....

Other things you can do when working with Enterprise Wikis:

- Collaborate on wiki pages with other users
- Comment on a wiki page to enable discussion about the contents of the page
- Rate a wiki page to share your opinion about its content
- Categorize wiki pages to enable users to quickly find information and share it with others

Group Work Site

This template provides a groupware solution that enables teams to create, organize, and share information quickly and easily. It includes Group Calendar, Circulation, Phone-Call Memo, the Document Library and the other basic lists.

The Group Work Site template produces what some might describe as one of the noisiest home pages of the available site templates (see Figure 11-20). When you create one of these sites, you'll find that you get a calendar, a tasks list, a links list, a team discussion list, and a lot more.

Team Site

A site for teams to quickly organize, author, and share information. It provides a document library, and lists for managing announcements, calendar items, tasks, and discussions.

Team sites might be the most popular type of site in SharePoint. In fact, when people describe SharePoint, they are often describing the functionality found within a team site. When you create a team site, you'll find elements such as a document library, named Shared Documents, and a tasks list added for you.

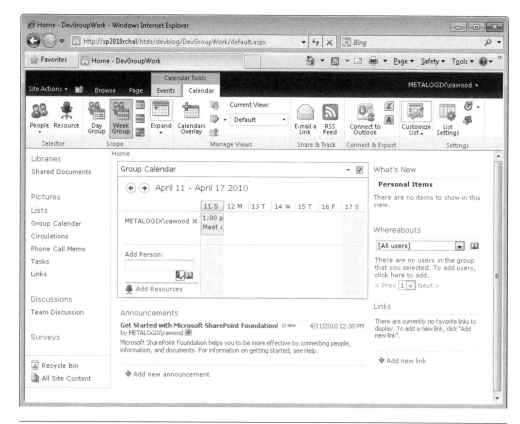

FIGURE 11-20   A new group work site

Content

When Microsoft Office SharePoint Server 2007 was released, one of the main improvements in the platform was the addition of publishing functionality that was previously found only in Microsoft Content Management Server. In SharePoint Server 2010, more has been added, and this is probably why the new Silverlight Create dialog offers a Content category instead of the previous name, Publishing.

Blog

A site for a person or team to post ideas, observations, and expertise that site visitors can comment on.

Blogs have become very popular over the last few years. They are discussed in detail in Chapter 4.

Document Center

A site to centrally manage documents in your enterprise.

The best features of SharePoint document management can be found in the Document Center site template. As the home page explains, "Use this site to create, work on, and store documents. This site can become a collaborative repository for authoring documents within a team, or a knowledge base for documents across multiple teams."

Publishing Site

A blank site for expanding your Web site and quickly publishing Web pages. Contributors can work on draft versions of pages and publish them to make them visible to readers. The site includes document and image libraries for storing Web publishing assets.

Publishing site templates are discussed in Chapter 6.

Publishing Site with Workflow

A site for publishing Web pages on a schedule by using approval workflows. It includes document and image libraries for storing Web publishing assets. By default, only sites with this template can be created under this site.

If you would like to add some more structure to your publishing experience, you might want to create a publishing site with workflow instead of a regular publishing site. As the name implies, edits under this type of site will need to be approved by a user who has sufficient rights.

If you created your initial site collection using the Publishing Site with Workflow template or the Collaboration Portal template, you will get these options. This template is often used for public-facing websites; one reason for this is that it provides for caching of content, so that the page loads faster.

Visio Process Repository

A site for teams to quickly view, share, and store Visio process diagrams. It provides a versioned document library for storing process diagrams, and lists for managing announcements, tasks, and review discussions.

This site template is reminiscent of the Document Center, but it is tailored to groups that work with Visio Process diagrams.

Meetings

Meeting sites are specifically designed to help SharePoint users manage meetings— usually with recurring meeting in mind. Whether you need to track meeting attendees, meeting goals, or some other data, meetings sites are meant to help ease the workload.

These sites can also be created right from within Microsoft Outlook so that you can schedule a meeting (or recurring meeting) and define the space to meet in, in one quick step. Meeting workspaces are discussed in Chapter 4.

Basic Meeting Workspace

A site to plan, organize, and capture the results of a meeting. It provides lists for managing the agenda, meeting attendees, and documents.

Blank Meeting Workspace

A blank meeting site for you to customize based on your requirements.

This workspace gives you the option of deciding what type of lists you would like to add.

Decision Meeting Workspace

A site for meetings that track status or make decisions. It provides lists for creating tasks, storing documents, and recording decisions.

This type of workspace is customized for the process of making decisions.

Multipage Meeting Workspace

A site to plan, organize, and capture the results of a meeting. It provides lists for managing the agenda and meeting attendees in addition to two blank pages for you to customize based on your requirements.

The Multipage Meeting Workspace is sort of the Meeting Workspace template on steroids. Using this type of site template, you get more out of the box.

Social Meeting Workspace

A site to plan social occasions. It provides lists for tracking attendees, providing directions, and storing pictures of the event.

If you're planning a social event with other people, a Social Meeting Workspace is probably right for the task

Web Databases

Obviously, databases are very powerful—after all, they power SharePoint on the back end. The web database site templates allow end users to create Microsoft Access databases through the SharePoint web interface. Using an Access database gives you the benefit of being able to leverage the many features of Access. Simply choose to open the database in Access when you need to use features only available in this rich client.

An interesting aspect of the web database templates is that you get some out-of-the-box help videos when you use them to create a site (see Figure 11-21). These videos provide help with configuring the database and using the database. If you're interested in these site templates, make sure to check out these short videos.

Assets Web Database

Create an assets database to keep track of assets, including asset details and owners.

This site template allows you to create a rich database for storing information about various assets you'd like to catalog.

Charitable Contributions Web Database

Create a database to track information about fundraising campaigns including donations made by contributors, campaign related events, and pending tasks.

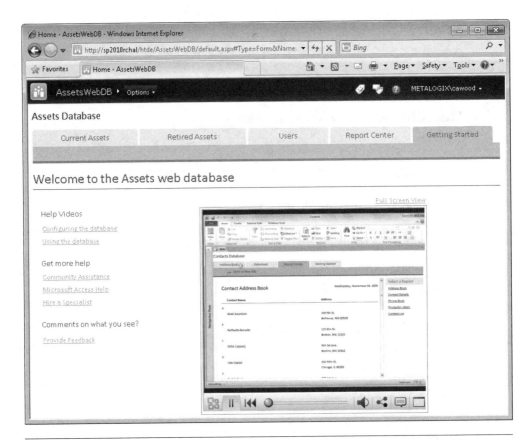

FIGURE 11-21 A help video in an Assets Web Database site

This site template is similar to the Assets Web Database site template, but it is customized for storing information about charitable contributions.

Contacts Web Database

Create a contacts database to manage information about people that your team works with, such as customers and partners.

Need a database of contacts? The Contacts Web Database site template is the place to start. While it's true that SharePoint also offers the Contact List type, the Contacts Web Database gives you the flexibility of using the reports that come with this site template and all of the Microsoft Access functionality.

Issues Web Database

Create an issues database to manage a set of issues or problems. You can assign, prioritize, and follow the progress of issues from start to finish.

The Issues Web Database allows you to track metrics such as the status, priority, and ownership of issues in the database.

Projects Web Database

Create a project tracking database to track multiple projects, and assign tasks to different people.

The Projects Web Database tracks such useful information as start date, end date, tasks, and attachments. If you switch to the Report Center tab, you can view reports such as Active Tasks and Project History.

Data

The only site template that fits into the Data category is the Records Center template.

Records Center

This template creates a site designed for records management. Records managers can configure the routing table to direct incoming files to specific locations. The site also lets you manage whether records can be deleted or modified after they are added to the repository.

The default content on the home page of a new Records Center site, listed next, encourages you to use the page to educate your colleagues about the records compliance policies of your organization:

Add links to other organizational compliance sites, such as:

- The definition of a record in your organization
- What happens to a record after it is submitted to the Records Center
- Steps users can take to comply with organizational policy

Add information about records management topics, such as:

- Your organization's compliance training site
- A site about organizational retention policies
- A list of records management contacts for each department

Search

The Search category of site templates contains templates that serve the needs of companies with enterprise search requirements.

Basic Search Center

A site for delivering the search experience. The site includes pages for search results and advanced searches.

If you don't need the customization options in the Enterprise Search Center, you might find that the Basic Search Center site template suits your needs.

Enterprise Search Center

A site for delivering the search experience. The welcome page includes a search box with two tabs: one for general searches, and another for searches for information about people. You can add and customize tabs to focus on other search scopes or result types.

As the description mentions, when you create a new Enterprise Search Center site, you'll get a general search box and another for a people search. However, you can add your own custom tabs and also use the advanced options to filter your result sets (see Figure 11-22).

FAST Search Center

A site for delivering the FAST search experience. The welcome page includes a search box with two tabs: one for general searches, and another for searches for information about people. You can add and customize tabs to focus on other search scopes or result types.

If your company is using the FAST search technology, you can use this site template as the basis for your customized search experience.

That's the end of the list of lists (and sites) and also the end of this book. I hope that you found it useful.

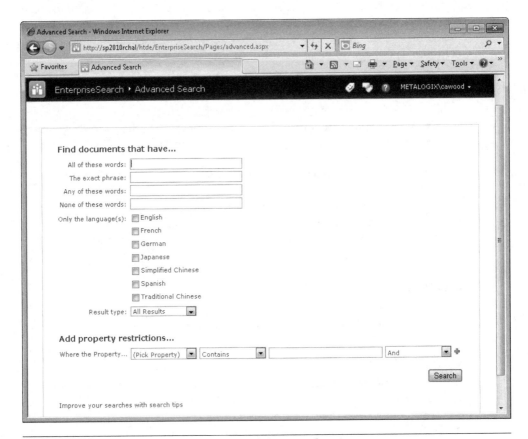

FIGURE 11-22 The advanced options of the search center

Index

Practical Guides for Microsoft SharePoint 2010 Users of Every Level

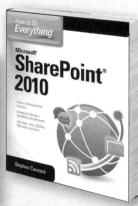

Learn more. **Mc Graw Hill** Do more.

MHPROFESSIONAL.COM

Available everywhere books are sold, in print and ebook formats.